Two Screenplays

Sticking Place Books 2026
© Michael Elias/Neversink Productions
© The Estate of Eve Babitz

ISBN 979-8-89976-077-8

Two Screenplays

Eve Babitz
and
Michael Elias

Sticking Place Books
New York

Introduction by Michael Elias

We met at Salvador Dalí's 1968 exhibit at Huntington Hartford's Columbus Circle Museum, both of us in near-anonymous New York youth. Eve's first fame was posing bare-breasted as "Miss Slum Goddess" on the cover of the *East Village Other*. Mine was more modest: a group photograph in *The New York Times*, sitting in a paddy wagon on the way to West Street Federal Penitentiary with my fellow actors from The Living Theatre's *The Brig*—we had been arrested in a sit-in protesting the closing of the theatre after the Becks refused to pay federal tax on ticket sales as a protest against the war machine. A protest wrapped in a protest. Eve, by contrast, was merely beautiful.

That evening we stood beside Dalí, admiring a painting, as his pet ocelot, Babou, draped around his neck, vomited on his satin jacket. We thought it was hilarious but, out of respect for a great artist, moved away to laugh. One thing led to another. A few days later we met for lunch at a Ukrainian pirogi café in the East Village, where Eve gave me her parents' phone number in Los Angeles and said, "If ever…"

The "if ever" came a year later at The Troubadour, between Eagle sets. "Of course I remember you," she said. "It was with Salvador Dalí and that disgusting animal." Then she introduced me to Glenn Frey.

I didn't see much more of Frey, but Eve took me to Ports, a small, gloriously disreputable restaurant on Santa Monica Boulevard where you were allowed to be odd, not a celebrity, and behind on your rent. Freddie Redd played the piano, Ronee Blakley sang, people recited poetry, staged short plays, or danced on whatever they had snorted or smoked in the bathroom. Once, Jimmy Gitter demanded questions in preparation for a *Jeopardy* audition. Jacques poured drinks for himself and the customers while his wife Micaela cooked in the tiny kitchen.

Eve invited me to her parents' house on Wilton Place for Thanksgiving. Her sister Mirandi made me a green leather rehearsal jacket modeled after Bertolt Brecht's. Sol and Mae Babitz became family to a New York boy in faraway Los Angeles. Our friendship—cemented there—would last.

At one point, in the middle of all that, I found myself in the dumpster of divorce: miserable, depressed, and not much fun to be around. Eve, struggling through the early days of AA, decided that the solution—for both of us—was to write a screenplay.

In the end, we wrote two.

The first was her idea.

"It will be a romantic comedy," she said, "about you. A heartbroken Hollywood writer who finds redemption and happiness by learning to play a musical instrument. Then he falls in love with his teacher."

"I used to play the trombone."

"A boy's instrument. It will be a flute."

It was better not to argue with Eve. There was always an air of finality—like when I would read something she'd written and say, "It's really good," and she'd reply, "Yes, I know."

"Okay," I said. "A flute."

"And we'll set it in Paris," she added, "so we can go there and watch them shoot it."

"A French movie? I don't speak French."

"We'll make him American. Like Gene Kelly. His wife will be French, she leaves him, and he meets someone like Leslie Caron. We'll start tomorrow."

Eve was fast and fearless. We outlined quickly, crammed as much of our lives into the story as we could—and then, in a way that felt inevitable, began to live it. Eve's father knew a flautist who gave me flute lessons; she took me to an enchanted cottage in Laurel Canyon where I bought a flute from a heart surgeon who collected them. "I'm selling you a used Gemeinhardt," he said. "If you get serious, we can discuss a Brannen."

We wrote scenes, assigned them to each other, rewrote each other's work, and somewhere in that process ended up with a respectable first draft.

Eve had met a French director at Ports, Roger Andrieux. He liked the script, took it back to Paris, and—as auteur directors do—completely rewrote it. Our witty Gene Kelly hero became a grouchy Frenchman. The title became *Envoyez les violons.*

I saw it on the Champs-Élysées without subtitles. I brought a VHS tape back to Los Angeles for Eve. We watched it on my Betamax. Neither of us understood a word. It bears some resemblance to our screenplay, but it's Andrieux's vision, not ours—a screenwriter's lament. Eve said our experience would make a funny episode of *Fantasy Island* where Ricardo Montalban gives a screenwriter a chance to remake his movie as it was originally written. Fat chance. Read ours. If you see the movie, you'll see.

The second script was *Remember Pearl Harbor,* set in Hollywood at the end of World War II—a romance between a Pasadena war widow and a screenwriter whose career is threatened by the return of real war heroes. This was Eve's world. She knew it in ways I never could: the menu at Musso & Frank, the rhythms of Hollywood, the small deceptions people lived inside, even a quack eye therapy that claimed to cure myopia. We used film noir tropes, our hero was 4-F by virtue of a surfing injury, set scenes in Tiajuana, and Eve promised not to show it to French directors.

These screenplays we wrote in the late 1980s are what remains of that collaboration. Reading these pages again is also, for me, a way of spending a little more time with Eve. And, reminding myself, that as Eve predicted, writing together would be fun, curative and despite the disappointment of the first, and the unsold state of the second we came out of the experience better than we were going in. And if, by some miracle, a producer, director, or star wanders in and decides to make one of them close to the way we wrote it—we've already picked out seats at the Egyptian.

Remember Pearl Harbor

Screenplay by Eve Babitz and Michael Elias

FADE IN:

SUPERIMPOSE: HOLLYWOOD 1945

FULL CLOSEUP - JULIE LIDO

A beautiful twenty-three-year-old starlet, raises a
mother-of-pearl opera glass and she could be Grace Kelly
at the ballet. But as the CAMERA PULLS BACK, we realize
she's in Rosenblatt's Fine Jewelry on Hollywood
Boulevard, staring across the street at the shoeshine
parlor through the rain. It is August, 1945.

                    JULIE
          Too bad it's only a movie, Jasper.
          Could I take these to the track?

At the mention of "track," the only other customer in the
store, Jasper Starkey, about thirty years -- a guy who
looks like he goes to the track, glances up from a
trayful of jewels. He's still wearing a jeweler's
eyepiece.

                    JASPER
          Not with me, sweetie-pie.

ROSENBLATT takes out a whole trayful of earrings,
necklaces, etc. They glitter like the real thing.

                    ROSENBLATT
          I can let you have these for
          fifteen dollars. If you want
          them insured, it's an extra
          dollar.

                    JULIE
          Oh, these are nice. Who designs
          these?

                    ROSENBLATT
          Cartier, Tiffany, all the big
          guys. (to Jasper; as Julie
          admires herself, trying on
          jewelry)
          A guy gives a girl the real thing,
          and she comes in here, sells it
          to me. When he says why don't you
          wear the earrings, she's got 'em.
          Reproduced. And the guy's gotta
          have one of these --
                    (indicates the loupe)
                    (MORE)

                    ROSENBLATT (CONT'D)
          -- and know what to look for, to
          tell the difference.

                         JASPER
          Who does this, chorus girls?

                       ROSENBLATT
          You kidding? Rich ladies who need
          cash in a hurry. I just finished a
          beauty.

He reaches under the counter and pulls out two identical
diamond and ruby necklaces, which look like a king's
ransom. They are in identical cases lined with black
velvet.

                       ROSENBLATT (CONT'D)
          The one on the left retails for
          fifty thousand. The one on the
          right, a hundred bucks
          (looks at them again, puzzled)
          Or maybe it's the one on the left.
          I'm getting real good.

                         JULIE
          Jasper, what do you think?

Julie is now bejeweled in seventy-five dollars' worth of
jewelry -- with her raincoat on -- and looks beautiful.
He looks at her through the opera glasses.

                         JASPER
          Like a million bucks.
               (to Rosenblatt, as he
                reaches for his
                wallet)
          I'll get that.
               (pays Rosenblatt)
          What the hell, the war's over.
          Everything is going to be
          wonderful now.

JASPER'S POV

The framed picture of a young man in an Army uniform
hangs on the wall behind the cash register. A black
ribbon decorates one corner.

ANGLE - ROSENBLATT

                       ROSENBLATT
          Yeah, wonderful.

INT. JASPER'S OFFICE - DAY

Jasper is at his desk, writing studiously, with intense
concentration, as he revises in longhand. There is
another desk, a typewriter, a couch, a dart board with a
picture of Hitler on it, and a few movie posters. If this
is not enough to place us in a writer's office at a major
Hollywood studio, the view THROUGH the window could make
the difference.

The door opens and MONTE PALMER steps in. He is wearing
evening clothes. Quite well, too. He is older than Jasper
and if he has an English accent, that's all right, too.

                    MONTE
              (sitting on his desk)
          'Morning, lad. Lovely day. I see
          you're off to a fine start. How
          are we?

                    JASPER
          You're late. I'm working on my
          book. More importantly, I've
          narrowed lunch down to Musso's,
          the Derby, or Mack's Chili Parlor.

                    MONTE
          Love a bowl of chili.
          Unfortunately, I'm not dressed for
          Mack's. Specials?

                    JASPER
          Tuesday: Corned beef and cabbage
          at Musso's, and the chicken salad
          at the Derby.

                    MONTE
          I despise chicken salad.

                    JASPER
          Then it's Mack's. I have an idea.

                    MONTE
          Oh?

                    JASPER
          It's about this screenwriter. The
          war is over and Tom Gerrard is
          returning to Hollywood to resume
          his career as the Colorado Kid.

                         JASPER (CONT'D)
              And unfortunately, this town is
              big enough for the both of us.

                         MONTE
              You were always his favorite
              writer.

                         JASPER
              I hate true stories.

Jasper looks out the window and sees Julie coming up the
walk. She pops her head in the window.

                         JULIE
              Lunch, anyone?

                         MONTE
              Mack's okay?

                         JULIE
              No. I have to be seen.

                         JASPER
              At lunch?

                         JULIE
              Let me put it this way. I don't
              want to be caught with a man in
              a tuxedo at a chili parlor at
              noon. I'm just not that kind of
              girl.

EXT. STREET - DAY

A huge estate in Pasadena: ESTABLISH the size and beauty
of the house, the gardens, the tennis courts, the
stables, and then in an alley behind it all a parked 1937
Plymouth. Next to it we see the back of a man, peering
through the bushes, and then:

MAN'S POV

Patricia Bevins -- gorgeous and twenty-four years old.
She's wearing a huge white terrycloth beach robe and
glasses. Regular glasses, not sunglasses. She steps to
the edge of the pool, takes off the robe and the glasses.
Then she has to feel around for her bathing cap because,
without her glasses, she's legally blind. She puts on the
bathing cap, slips into the pool, and begins swimming
laps.

ANGLE - MRS. QUARTERMAINE

An eighty-year-old Victorian grande dame, sits at an
umbrella-table reading her newspaper.

The butler, ANDREW, arrives a moment later with a tray of
iced tea, which he sets down beside her. Andrew is
wearing a white butler's uniform.

Patricia is oblivious to all this. She is just swimming
as though it is a common occurrence for her great aunt to
watch her swim. Patricia raises her head for a moment.

PATRICIA'S POV

We see how OUT OF FOCUS her aunt, the butler, and the
whole iced tea situation is to her.

There is an air of ominousness about all of this as we
RETURN TO:

STRANGER'S POV

Hiding and watching from the bushes.

EXT. GARDEN OF ALLAH POOL - DAY

This pool is not ominous. It is surrounded by "Garden of
Allah" types: writers, actors, jazz musicians, soldiers
and Navy boys, hookers and starlets. It's a swell place.

A YOUNG SAILOR plops down next to Jasper on a pool chair.

                    SAILOR
          Got a cigarette?

                    JASPER
          Help yourself, Myron. How about a
          drink?

                    SAILOR
          I think I drank enough last night.

                    JASPER
          You still love her?

                    SAILOR
          Yeah, but she threw me out.

                    JASPER
          What now?

                    SAILOR
          I guess I go back to Montana and
          teach algebra.

                    JASPER
          How much do you need?

                    SAILOR
          Train fare.

                    JASPER
              (handing him a
               hundred-dollar bill)
          Will this do it?

                    SAILOR
          Oh, yeah. Gee, Montana sure is
          going to look funny after all
          this. You're okay, Jasper.

                    JASPER
          Have a good trip.

Jasper watches the Sailor go. He resumes writing. He has
the same note pad he was using in his office.

Julie appears at the edge of the pool, carrying two
bunches of mail. She hands Jasper one of the bunches and
sits down where the Sailor was sitting so she can open
hers.

Jasper finds one envelope with the Quartermaine name
engraved on it and tears it open eagerly.

                    JASPER (CONT'D)
          (reading the letter) Ah,
          wonderful... wonderful!

EXT. PASADENA STREET - DAY

Jasper, in his 1939 red Cadillac convertible, is driving
past the staid, old mansions of Pasadena. The trees are
old, the homes are stately, and the atmosphere is
altogether un-red-Cadillac-convertible-y.

In front of the stateliest mansion of them all, Jasper
arrives and we watch as he tries to decide whether to
park in the gigantic, circular driveway or on the street
like the commoner he is.

He parks on the street. Gets out of the car and starts to
walk.

This is the first time we notice Jasper has a little
limp.

Jasper rings the portentous doorbell. A moment later,
Andrew, the butler opens it.

                    ANDREW
          Yes?

                    JASPER
          I'm Jasper Starkey.

INT. HOUSE - DAY

Jasper follows Andrew through the house, which is opulent
and dark, into the library.

                    ANDREW
          This is the library. If there's a
          problem, I will be glad to help,
          but I am sure everything is in
          order. Mrs. Quartermaine insists
          that the library be available only
          between nine and four, and no
          books are to be removed from the
          premises. You may smoke on the
          patio through those French doors.
          Will there be anything else?

                    JASPER
          Please thank Mrs. Quartermaine for
          me.

                    ANDREW
          What did you say your area of
          California was, sir?

                    JASPER
          Pioneer merchants of Tulare
          County. I'm a native son, you
          know.

Andrew retires, and Jasper, now that he's inside, doesn't
know what to do, so he starts looking at books. But, like
a kid in school, he starts idly staring out the window.
The window overlooks the front drive. Suddenly, he
squints and perks up.

JASPER'S POV

FROM two blocks away, we see three beautiful young WOMEN
in tennis clothes, on bicycles.

The girls stop just under the window and don't see him.
He listens to their conversation.

                         PATRICIA
          You can't stay for a swim?

                         CAROLYN
          Mother's having the Rose Committee
          over. This year's going to be a
          big one, I guess.

                         MARILYN
               (Carolyn's twin)
          And we have to pour. But maybe we
          can stay later next Wednesday,
          because --

                         CAROLYN
          -- The committee will be all
          formed.

Patricia waves goodbye and goes inside.

BACK TO SCENE

This leaves Jasper with nothing to do again, so he opens
his briefcase on the desk and takes out a pad and
pencils. Then he lights a cigar.

At this point, a four-year-old kid, Skipper, appears in
the doorway holding a ball, looking with curiosity at
Jasper.

                         JASPER
          Give me the ashtray over there,
          okay, kid?

The kid lifts the heavy ashtray and brings it to Jasper.
Jasper lets the kid stand holding the ashtray as he
flicks ashes into it.

                         JASPER (CONT'D)
          What's your name?

                         SKIPPER
          Skipper.

                         JASPER
          What are you doing here?

                         SKIPPER
          I live here. What are you doing
          here?

                    JASPER
          Research for a novel. You know
          what a novel is?

                    SKIPPER
          No.

Patricia comes in from the hall, looking for Skipper.
Skipper ducks under the desk where Jasper is sitting.

Patricia is still in her tennis clothes. Jasper perks up
at the sight of her, while remembering that he's got
Skipper under his desk.

                    PATRICIA
          Have you seen a little boy?

                    JASPER
          How little?

                    PATRICIA
          Little enough to fit under a desk.

Skipper squeals with delight, but both adults enjoy
playing dumb a while longer.

                    JASPER
          No one's that little.

Skipper is now hysterical with laughter.

                    PATRICIA
          Maybe you're right.

                    JASPER
          You might try the closet.

Patricia, with exaggerated earnestness, looks in the
closet.

                    PATRICIA
          Nothing in there.

While she's looking, Skipper squeals and zips out, to
hide behind the couch.

                    PATRICIA (CONT'D)
          If you don't mind, I'll look under
          the desk.

                    JASPER
              (winking at Skipper)
              Nothing here.

He shows her.

While Patricia makes a thorough search under the desk,
her glasses drop off and, as she rises without them,
Jasper, who's stood up to help her look, says:

                    JASPER (CONT'D)
          Why, Miss Jones, you're beautiful.

                    PATRICIA
          I know, but I can't see and my
          name's not Miss Jones. I'm
          Patricia Bevens.
                  (puts glasses back
                   on)
          Who are you?

                    JASPER
          Jasper Starkey. I'll be doing
          research here. You know, you're
          even beautiful with your glasses
          on.

                    PATRICIA
          Oh, yes. You're the writer. Do you
          play tennis?

                    JASPER
          Limp.

                    PATRICIA
          Oh, I'm sorry, the war?

                    JASPER
          Falling headlong.

                    PATRICIA
          Falling? Headlong?

                    JASPER
          In love with you. Anyway, that's
          how I wish it happened.

                    PATRICIA
              (snubs him)
          Mr. Starkey, you go too far.

She puts her glasses on.

                    PATRICIA (CONT'D)
          How were you injured, if it's not
          too personal?

                    JASPER
          It's personal.

She is re-snubbed, having snubbed him.

Skipper now bursts out from behind the couch and begins
circling the globe, screaming with joy at the top of his
lungs.

                    PATRICIA
          There he is!
               (straightens up)
          So, you're using the library.

                    JASPER
          If you don't mind, Bevens.

She looks at him now and smiles.

                    PATRICIA
          No, I don't mind. In fact, maybe
          when you're done with -- whatever
          it is you're doing, you might like
          some tea.

                    JASPER
          Tea?

                    PATRICIA
          Or coffee.

                    JASPER
          For two?

                    PATRICIA
          At three.

INT. JASPER'S APARTMENT - NIGHT

This is a typical, shabby Garden of Allah bungalow, done
in cocoa. We see evidence of a misspent Hollywood life --
towels, a typewriter, cluttered dinner table, index
cards, bulletin board against a wall overladen with
bills, story ideas, and girl friends' notes. Also, his
bed is so covered with books that there's an outline of
where he sleeps on the side near the lamp.

We also see some beer bottles, cards, old racing forms,
binoculars, poker chips, a poker table with a cat asleep
in the middle, a bottle of Pepto Bismol, and a lot of
magazines, <u>Saturday Evening Posts</u>, <u>Colliers</u>, and
<u>Esquires</u>. A "Vargas" girl hangs over the fake fire-place,
and on the mantle is an Oscar, lying on its side. On a
coat hanger are a bunch of hats, a couple of canes, an
actual coat and a Colt .45 in a cowboy holster.

Jasper hangs the phone up and looks at the Vargas girl,
in satin teddies, reclining on a mauve chaise. He picks
up a pencil and draws glasses on her. Now she looks like
Patricia. Jasper steps back, pleased as punch.

                    JASPER
          (sighing) Perfect.

He steps forward, cocks his head, and draws the glasses
better -- even more incongruous with the pin-up pose.

                    JASPER (CONT'D)
          Hubba-hubba.

Jasper's door is closed, but we can hear everything
outside anyway, since the walls are paper thin. Only now,
we recognize Julie's voice and the baritone voice of a
man she's with. His name is Hugh Green.

                    JULIE (O.S.)
          What are you doing?

                    HUGH (O.S.)
          I'm trying to unzip your dress.

                    JULIE (O.S.)
          Why?

                    HUGH (O.S.)
          So it won't get wrinkled.

                    JULIE (O.S.)
          I have a five o'clock call.

                    HUGH (O.S.)
          Let's go inside and have a drink
          and talk about this.

                    JULIE (O.S.)
          This is not a date, you idiot.
          Publicity fixed us up for the
          premiere. Stop unzipping me!

                    HUGH (O.S.)
          But I like you.

                    JULIA (O.S.)
          What has that got to do with it?

Jasper opens the door.

                    JASPER
          Hi, kids. How was the movie?
           (to Julie)
          Did you get my cigarettes?

HUGH is now off balance, fumbling in his pockets.

                    HUGH
          What do you smoke?

                    JULIE
          Dear, this is Hugh Green, my date.
          Mister Green, this is Jasper
          Starkey, the boy next door.

                    HUGH
          I thought you lived here.

                    JULIE
          With him?
                (shrugs, shakes
                 her head; turns to
                  Hugh and shakes his
                  hand)
          I had a lovely time.

Jasper takes three of Hugh's cigarettes.

                    HUGH
          Didn't you write <u>Mrs. Miniver</u>?

                    JULIE
          Him? No, he wrote...

                    HUGH
          Oh, yeah, the French, uh --

                    JASPER
          That's the one.

                    JULIE
          You want to see his Oscar?

                    HUGH
                (to both of them)
          I don't think so. Nice meeting
          you.

Hugh bows out.

INT. JASPER'S APARTMENT - NIGHT

Julie, dressed in fake jewels and a dress from wardrobe
for the premiere, enters, looking entirely at home, as
she fixes herself a Bromo Seltzer. She takes off her
shoes and stockings -- with garter belt for atmosphere.

She looks at Jasper as he lights her cigarette. Jasper is
obviously not himself. She sips her Bromo Seltzer.

                    JULIE
          Do you want to hear about the
          picture?

                    JASPER
          I don't think so. Monte and I did
          two weeks on it. I only wish it
          ill.

Julie wanders in front of the fireplace and picks up the
pencil that Jasper was using to draw glasses on the
Vargas girl.

                    JULIE
              (about to draw on
               her)
          How about a moustache?

                    JASPER
          No, I like it like that.
              (pauses)
          She lives in Pasadena with her
          aunt. Can you believe she's a
          widow? With a kid?

Julie has begun to get undressed, and it is obvious that
they are on very friendly terms. Or were. She zips her
self back up, getting the point.

                    JULIE
          Does this mean I'm de trop?

                    JASPER
          What does that mean?

                    JULIE
          Cramping your style?

                    JASPER
          Look, I don't know. I don't
          know... I'll ask you for the last
          time, let's get married.

                    JULIE
          Jasper, I didn't come to Hollywood
          to get married. I came to have
          cheap affairs and get rich and
          famous and make everybody jealous
          in Pawtucket. If you want to get
          married, anything east of La Brea
          is more like it. Here there are
          people naked in the pool, not
          getting married.

                    JASPER
          They say they're engaged.

                    JULIE
          Engorged, not engaged.

                    JASPER
          You take those Marx brothers too
          seriously.

                    JULIE
          Well, let's play gin.

Like an old married couple, they shoo the cat off the
poker table and while away the night.

There they sit, she in her premiere drag, and he in his
race track Charlie attire, very seriously settling in for
a deadly gin game.

So much for sex.

EXT. PASADENA MANSION - DAY

Jasper pulls up in his red Cadillac, only this time he
parks in the driveway.

EXT. GROUNDS - SOMEONE'S POV - DAY

About fifty feet away from Jasper. Through a clump of
oleander bushes. He sees Jasper get out of the car and
enter the house.

INT. LIBRARY - DAY

We see Jasper working, taking notes at a table, a pile of
books at his side. Suddenly bored, he gets up.

EXT. GROUNDS - DAY

Jasper is smoking and walking.

He passes the greenhouse and then the garages, and Andrew
polishing one of the cars.

                    JASPER
          How're you doing, chief?

                    ANDREW
          Almost finished.

                    JASPER
          Wouldn't figure the Quartermaines
          for a Ford.

                    ANDREW
          It's mine, sir. I haven't taken it
          out much since the gas rations,
          but I'm hoping, with the war over,
          I can visit my sister in Oakland.
          How's your work coming?

                    JASPER
          It's going to be a long time
          before I really understand the
          Gold Rush.

                    ANDREW
          What's so difficult to understand,
          sir?

                    JASPER
          It wasn't just the money. It was
          something else. Maybe just the
          adventure.

                    ANDREW
          Like the Army, sir, wouldn't you
          say?

                    JASPER
          Did you know Skipper's father?

                    ANDREW
          Mark Bevens, sir? I'm sorry. He
          was never in this house. He was
          killed at Pearl Harbor. Sent there
          just a few weeks after they were
          married. Shame he never came
          back.

EXT. HOLLYWOOD BUNGALOW HOUSE - DAY

Jasper parks and takes a bag of groceries up the front
steps, stopping a moment while he fits the key into the
front door.

There is a sign in the window of this bungalow which
reads: "REGINA STARKEY -- BATES METHOD -- SIGHT WITHOUT
GLASSES."

INT. BUNGALOW - DAY

The house is darkened as we hear voices in the living
room, while Jasper goes back into the kitchen.

                    REGINA (O.5.)
          Blink, blink, blink, blink. Now
          breathe quietly, deeply... now
          blink, blink, blink, blink.

In the kitchen, Jasper puts the groceries down on the
counter and opens the refrigerator to put stuff away. He
sees a meatloaf and removes it.

                    REGINA (O.5.) (CONT'D)
          All right. Now the balls.

Jasper's got a piece of meatloaf in hand and quietly
walks to the hall, parts the curtains, and peeps in.

JASPER'S POV

In the darkened room, a woman is juggling two tennis
balls, blinking and breathing. Watching is REGINA
STARKEY, a woman in her prime with flaming red hair,
dressed like a Gibson girl. All over the room are eye
charts, a plaster of Paris eye, a parakeet in a cage, and
black velvet curtains.

INT. KITCHEN - LATER

Jasper is eating his sandwich. There's a KNOCK at the
back door. Jasper opens it and sees a young man (JIMMY)
who at first doesn't recognize him, and vice versa.

                    JIMMY
          Oh... it's me, Mister Starkey.
          Jimmy, from next door. I'm home.

                    JASPER
          Jesus, Jimmy, I'm sorry. Come on
          in. You look great.

                    JIMMY
          I saw your car out front and I
          thought I'd come by and say hello.
          It's been three years.

                    JASPER
          Want some meatloaf?

While Jasper makes Jimmy a sandwich, their conversation
continues. During which Jimmy eats the entire meatloaf.

Mrs. Starkey enters.

                    REGINA
               (hugging Jimmy)
          Doesn't he look wonderful? Grown
          up, strong and slim...

                    JASPER
               (preoccupied; to
                Regina)
          Listen, what's it like being
          blind?

                    REGINA
          You mean, really blind?

                    JASPER
          No... but I think I'm in love with
          this girl and her glasses are this
          thick.

                    REGINA
          Send her over here. Immediately.

                    JASPER
          She's in Pasadena.

                    REGINA
          So, that's why you keep going
          there. Novel hah.

                    JASPER
          She's an innocent fringe benefit
          bystander.

Front BELL RINGS.

                    REGINA
          There's my three o'clock.

Regina exits.

                    JASPER
          So, what do you think you'll do
          now?

                    JIMMY
          I'm waiting for my brother to come
          back from the Philippines so we
          can open our store. You know, I
          had this girl friend the whole
          time I was in German prison camp,
          and I just imagined how it would
          be with   her when I came home.
          You know, the two years I spent in
          prison camp, I was with older
          guys, sophisticated... She's just
          a kid, still. She talks about
          movie stars all the time. She
          wants to go ice skating. I mean, I
          saw guys die -- starve to death --
          they had Russian prisoners in our
          camp; those guys dropped like
          flies. And now, with my old girl
          friend, it's amazing. We're both
          the same age -- twenty-one -- I
          guess I'll get used to it. At
          least your mother's meatloaf is
          how I remembered it.

                    JASPER
          Want some more?

                    JIMMY
          May I?

Jimmy cuts himself another huge slice and they eat in
silence as the RAIN comes down outside.

                    JASPER
          Coming home isn't easy, is it?

                    JIMMY
          I guess you could say I got mixed
          emotions.

INT. PATRICIA'S BEDROOM - DAY

Patricia's tennis clothes are on the bed. While we wait
for her to change, the CAMERA examines the room. On the
wall is an Annapolis pennant.

On her dresser is a photo of Patricia and Skipper in a
sailor suit, more   of Patricia, one showing her leaning
against a car next to a girl her age, a graduation photo,
on a horse jumping a fence, a girls' field hockey team,
and a baby picture of Skipper. Patricia enters the room.
She's wearing a white terrycloth robe and is stuffing her
hair into a bathing cap.

EXT. POOL - DAY

Lots of blue water, comfortable furniture, deserted
except for the elderly Susan Quartermaine dozing in the
sun on a chaise. Patricia comes down the path to the
pool, notices the sleeping woman, leaves   her
undisturbed, and walks around the pool to the deep end.
She removes her robe and glasses, places the glasses on
the diving board, and dives into the water.

EXT. MANSION - LAWN - DAY

Jasper is sitting on a wicker chair with a sketchbook
looking thing in his hand, apparently sketching Mrs.

Quartermaine seated on a wicker swing and looking very
beautiful, old-fashioned and nostalgic.

                    MRS. QUARTERMAINE
          You know, when we first came here,
          there was nothing -- no buildings,
          no people -- no Hollywood. It was
          the trains, you know, that made
          this place what it is. Most other
          cities, you know, start from
          seaports, but here, with us, it
          was trains. My husband's trains.

We see looking more closely at Jasper that he's not
drawing her, he's taking notes.

                    JASPER
          How much of this belongs to your
          lot?

                    MRS. QUARTERMAINE
          Our lot?

                    JASPER
          Your property.

                    MRS. QUARTERMAINE
          To those hills.

                         JASPER
               Those hills?

He indicates the purple mountains in the distance.

                         MRS. QUARTERMAINE
               Just to the top.

Jasper looks back from the mountains and finds himself
looking at Patricia who is walking with Skipper.

                         MRS. QUARTERMAINE (CONT'D)
               My niece... one of this country's
               first war widows.

                         JASPER
               I'm sorry.

                         MRS. QUARTERMAINE
               At least she has Skipper.

She searches his face for a reaction but there is none.

EXT. TRAIL - DAY

Jasper and Patricia are walking through a cactus garden
and down a road lined with eucalyptus.

                         PATRICIA
               I take classes.

                         JASPER
               What are you studying?

                         PATRICIA
               Oh, just the atom.

                         JASPER
               The atom. The one they made the
               bomb out of?

                         PATRICIA
               That's just it. I don't know what
               to think. I'm at a terrible time
               in my life right now. I used to
               think Fermi and Oppenheimer, those
               ... those physicists, were such
               giants... But now...

                         JASPER
               It ended the war.

                         PATRICIA
          I just don't respect them. You
          have to respect a man...

                         JASPER
          A man?

                         PATRICIA
          Well, there was one younger
          scientist -- we were
          corresponding.

                         JASPER
          Aha!

                         PATRICIA
          And now I'm disgusted with the
          whole subject!

                         JASPER
          That's it, isn't it?

                         PATRICIA
          What's it?

                         JASPER
          You think I'm cute but you don't
          respect me.

                         PATRICIA
          I don't even know if you're that
          cute.

They begin to laugh; but he's worried.

EXT. STUDIO - DAY

We see Monte and Jasper leave their office.

INT. COMMISSARY - DAY

Jasper and Monte are sitting in the commissary having
lunch.

                         JASPER
          I'm 4-F, I'm a screenwriter, I'm
          from Hollywood, I don't know an
          atom from an M&M -- no wonder she
          doesn't respect me.

                         MONTE
          Hell, I don't even respect you.

                    JASPER
          This is serious...

                    MONTE
          How are we going to get our gent
          our of there...

                    JASPER
          Let's have him slash the sail and
          slide down the rope to the
          foredeck...

                    MONTE
          This is the western.

                    JASPER
          Oh.

EXT. PASADENA - DAY

We see the whole beautiful "40s" place.

EXT. QUARTERMAINES' - DAY

We see Jasper's car parked in the driveway.

INT. QUARTERMAINES' LIBRARY - DAY

Up to his elbows in open books, Jasper is taking notes
and thinking, biting a pencil until it is shredded.

Looking out the French window, he can see clear through
the gardens to the mountains in the distance.

When he gets too bored, he gets this pair of binoculars
and sort of leans against the door and just is lost in
free-floating gazing.

Behind him now, is Andrew, who clears his throat.

                    ANDREW
          A-hem.

Jasper turns guiltily around.

                    JASPER
          Oh, I was just looking for uh... a
          match.

He quickly finds a cheap cigar in his pocket to expound
on this   excuse.

                         ANDREW
               A match, sir?

He begins to laugh.

                         JASPER
               How about a cigar?

                         JASPER (CONT'D)
               Not that I like these. Before the
               war you could really get great
               cigars, but now...

                         ANDREW
               Perhaps, I can help you...

INT. ROOM OFF LIBRARY

Andrew is showing Jasper an old humidor filled with great
cigars.

                         JASPER
               My God, these are real Cubanos. I
               thought they didn't make these
               anymore.

                         ANDREW
                    (helping himself to a
                     couple)
               They don't.

Andrew picks up an elegant lighter and lights both their
cigars.

They stand on a balcony and sigh.

As CAMERA BACKS AWAY we see Patricia on a chaise below.

TERRACE - MOMENTS LATER

Patricia on a chaise, Jasper sitting next to her.

                         JASPER
               How could Rudolph Valentino be his
               favorite actor?

                         PATRICIA
               The world is just like that
               sometimes. Thank goodness. Or
               things would really be boring.

                    JASPER
          Can I kiss you yet or what?

                    PATRICIA
          You are a terrible man, Mr.
          Starkey, and I don't know you very
          well but...

                    JASPER
          Your hands are shaking.

Jasper and Patricia are nearly touching each other face
to face.

                    JASPER (CONT'D)

          I'll wait.

                    PATRICIA
          Oh, now I'll dream of you at
          night.

                    JASPER
          But not much longer. Your hands,
          they're so cold.

                    PATRICIA
          That must mean, lucky in love.

EXT. QUARTERMAINE GARDENS

Jasper is wandering through the gardens, smoking his
cigar.

At the fishpond, Skipper is playing fisherman with a
small fishing pole. He also is sailing a boat on the
pond.

                    JASPER
          Good afternoon, Master Skipper.

                    SKIPPER
          Fish.

                    JASPER
          And boat.

                    SKIPPER
          Want to see my train?

Skipper leads Jasper by the hand.

They go through a small path and a large hedge and come
to a long building that looks like a garage.

Skipper tries to open the door to this garage but can't,
so Jasper does it.

INT. GARAGE

Inside this garage is a giant private railroad car
painted with gold and roses.

Jasper is totally stunned. Railroad tracks lead out the
back of this "garage" and this is obviously one of those
private cars people once took to get from place to place.

> SKIPPER
> Grandpa's.

Outside we hear a voice.

> PATRICIA
> Skipper?

Patricia enters, out of breath and gorgeous.

> JASPER
> I was expecting a Lionel.

> PATRICIA
> My grandfather and Diamond Jim
> Brady had this train competition
> -- they both had their own cars
> -- but I think Grandpa's was a lot
> less ostentatious.

Since this train is as ostentatious as we can imagine,
this is quite a fact.

> JASPER
> No kidding?

> PATRICIA
> A little.

She is mad at herself for slipping enough to kid him,
and obviously wishes she hadn't.

> PATRICIA (CONT'D)
> There are still old tracks where
> they could pick his train up out
> the back door.

                    JASPER
          No kidding?

It's true. Jasper looks at her.

                    PATRICIA
          Its true.

                    JASPER
          You know, my mother is an expert
          on vision. Can I see yours?

                    PATRICIA
          But I...

She does and Jasper holds them up to look at her
prescription.

INT. JASPER'S CAR - DAY

Jasper and Patricia are on their way to Hollywood.

EXT. JASPER'S MOTHER'S HOUSE - DAY

Jasper and Patricia enter his mother's house.

INT. REGINA'S EYE TREATMENT CLIENT ROOM

Patricia is being tested by Regina.

                    REGINA
          Only six months, maybe a year, you
          could throw away those glasses and
          see perfectly, now try this...

Regina throws Patricia a red ball.

                    PATRICIA
          You really think...

                    REGINA
          But you have to do your exercises
          every single day and keep your
          appointment with me once a week.

                    PATRICIA
          Gee, I...

                    REGINA
          When you're ready...

EXT. JASPER'S CAR

Driving back to Pasadena.

INT. CAR - DAY

Patricia is sort of dazed and enchanted.

                    PATRICIA
          Your mother's quite a hot tomato
          isn't she?

                    JASPER
          A what?

She pronounces this to-mah-to -

                    PATRICIA
          I mean, I can see where you get
          your...

                    JASPER
          My what?

                    PATRICIA
          Je ne sais quoi.

                    JASPER
          Humph.

Jasper shrugs, happy she's been reduced to French whether
he knows what it means or not.

                    JASPER (CONT'D)
          You're a pretty hot to-mah-to
          yourself, Mildred.

Patricia loves being called Mildred.

EXT. GARDEN OF ALLAH - NIGHT

It's a hot summer night. Julie and Monte and Jasper are
outside playing gin and drinking hi-balls.

                    MONTE
          Whole room full of cigars?

                    JASPER
          And a train.

                    JULIE
          Oh, those...

She motions tiny toy trains which she thinks Jasper
means.

                    JASPER
          No. With tracks. A real train
          -- like Diamond Jim Brady. Plus,
          she says to-mah-to.

                    JULIE
          He's in love.

                    MONTE
          Next thing you know, he's taking
          her home to mother's.

                    JASPER
          She's myopic.

                    MONTE
          He has taken her home to mother.

                    JULIE
          You mean she's...

                    JASPER
          Look, I took you home to mother
          and you don't wear glasses
          anymore, right? I was just...

Julie draws a final card, lays it down.

                    JULIE
          Gin, po-tah-to heads!!

Monte and Jasper are very non-plussed. Julie is obviously
a poor winner.

                    MONTE
          See what happens when they learn
          how to see?

INT. LIBRARY - DAY

Mrs. Quartermaine is seated at a desk, gluing corners on
a photo album to put pictures in.

Jasper is looking at some of the photos. One shows two
enormously fat men with napkins tied around their necks,
with huge piles of oysters on the table in front of them.

                         MRS. QUARTERMAINE
              My husband and Diamond Jim, one of
              their oyster contests... Of
              course, poor Charles never won.
              But by then we were so rich, it
              didn't matter... losing a gold
              mine, in a hand of poker or one of
              these games. Men! My Charles would
              play for anything... for fun or a
              good cause. The only thing he
              objected to was being cheated, you
              know, or someone trying to bully
              him. Like when they kidnapped me.

                         JASPER
              They what?

                         MRS. QUARTERMAINE
              If I didn't climb out the back
              window, I'd still be there -- he
              said not one cent
              for the bastards. And you know...

                         JASPER
              Yes.

                         MRS. QUARTERMAINE
              He was right.

                         JASPER
              But what if they...

                         MRS. QUARTERMAINE
              He was right. Not one red cent
              except for fun. Of course, in
              those days money meant something.
              Not like today. Fifteen cents for
              a loaf of bread, it's…

                         JASPER
              Outtlandish.

Mrs. Quartermaine begins to laugh, we can see how much
she likes Jasper.

                         MRS. QUARTERMAINE
              We did have fun. He would have
              liked you.

Mrs. Quartermaine hands Jasper a tray full of cookies.

                         JASPER
             Oh, boy, the chocolate kind.

ANGLE - POOL

Patricia glides under water.

Up for air. What she sees -- not much. Everything has
blurred edges. But vaguely she sees a man in a white
jacket approach the sleeping Mrs.Q

CLOSER ANGLE ON PATRICIA

As she starts her laps. She reaches out, touches the
wall, does a racing turn, and shoots back toward the deep
end of the pool.

PATRICIA'S POV

The blurred bottom of the pool. Then, the wall of the
deep end.

CLOSE ANGLE ON PATRICIA

Bubbles, swirling water, as she kicks herself off the
wall and begins her next lap.

ANGLE FROM HIGH ABOVE - POOL

We can see everything. Mrs.Q is asleep. Patricia   is
swimming toward her. The blue water is turning red from
blood pouring out of the knife wound in the Mrs. Qâ€™s
chest. The blood has run into the pool, and the pink at
the diluted farther edges gets redder. Patricia swims
into the pink.

PATRICIA'S POV

The cloudy, swirling pink water.

ANGLE - PATRICIA

She stands up and sees the blurred figure of her aunt,
leaking red blood into the pool.

We see Patricia's face as she again looks down into the
pool, seeing that she herself is soaking in this blood
and water combination. She shows shock and horror as she
starts to scream.

IT. LIBRARY

Jasper hears Patricia's screams and comes running down,
just in time to see a man in a white jacket, moving.

INT. HOUSE - NIGHT

In the library, seated here and there in a circle, are
the maid, the cook, Patricia, and Jasper. The POLICE
CHIEF and a DETECTIVE. The CHIEF looks very annoyed as
though he can't quite believe his ears, no matter how
often he hears it. NANNY is there, too.

                    POLICE CHIEF
               (long sigh)
          Okay. Now if you don't mind, I'd
          just like to know where everyone
          was between four and five this
          afternoon. Mrs. Wells...

                    PATRICIA
          Mrs. Wells... Nanny...

Mrs. Wells was upstairs with

Skipper, my son.

                    POLICE CHIEF
          Your son was in his room till five
          o'clock, and all you others were --

                    COOK
               (a calm, sweet lady
                with a face above
                suspicion)
          I have been with Mrs. Quartermaine
          for forty years, and at four
          o'clock I am always asleep,
          upstairs in my room, but I'm
          afraid I didn't hear anything.

She begins to cry.

                    POLICE CHIEF
          That's fine, don't worry.

Police Chief nods at the Maid.

                    MAID
          It's Thursday, isn't it?

                    POLICE CHIEF
          All day.

                    MAID
          It's my day off. I went to the
          movies. To <u>Waterloo Bridge</u>.

                    POLICE CHIEF
          With Robert Taylor?

                    MAID
               (offended) Tyrone
               Power.

                    POLICE CHIEF
          I could have sworn --

                    JASPER
          It was Tyrone Power.

Police Chief turns to Jasper.

                    JASPER (CONT'D)
          Four o'clock I'm at my desk, when
          I hear Patricia scream.

Police Chief turns to Patricia.

                    PATRICIA
          I was in the pool. Swimming. I
          looked up and saw... Andrew always
          brings my aunt her iced tea at
          four. And he did.

                    POLICE CHIEF
          And then?

                    PATRICIA
          The pool... the water...

She begins to cry, and Jasper hands her his manly
handkerchief.

                    POLICE CHIEF
          And Andrew and his car are
          missing. And the delivery boy says
          he saw him driving away. It seems
          rather obvious --

                    ACE DETECTIVE
          The butler did it?

Jasper flinches and looks like he just bit into a lemon.
Patricia stops crying and looks up.

                    PATRICIA
          Andrew is one of the family.

                    POLICE CHIEF
          It's usually a member of the
          family.

EXT. CALIFORNIA DRIVE-IN RESTAURANT - NIGHT

Jasper and Patricia are sitting in the car, Patricia is
eating lots and lots of French fries and a cheeseburger.

                    PATRICIA
          I thought, now that the war's
          over, things would be okay.
          But...

                    JASPER
          Did you think she'd live forever?

                    PATRICIA
          I thought I'd have a chance to say
          goodbye. Now it's too late.

                    JASPER
          Me, too. Damn it.

                    PATRICIA
          Now, now I have no one.

Jasper wipes catsup off her chin.

                    JASPER
          It's too late. You have me.

                    PATRICIA
          But...

                    JASPER
          It's too late. You do.

EXT. POOL - DAY

The Quartermaine pool is being drained.

INT. HOUSE - DAY

Patricia is scanning a bunch of newspapers. Standing next
to her is an austere Pasadena LAWYER. In the next room,
we hear sounds of Skipper playing.

                    LAWYER
          We were very fortunate. The police
          didn't want this in the papers,
          either.

                    PATRICIA
          Why not?

Skipper escapes from his nanny and rides his tricycle
into the room where Patricia is.

                    SKIPPER
          Honk! Honk!

He encircles his other and is out before she can scold
him.

                    LAWYER
          Pasadena has never had this kind
          of scandal.

                    PATRICIA
          Well, that's not the police's
          reason, is it?

                    LAWYER
          The police are employed by the
          city.

                    PATRICIA
          I don't quite see my aunt's murder
          as a scandal.

                    LAWYER
          They're trying to protect you.

                    PATRICIA
          Why me?

                    LAWYER
          Because you're a very rich woman,
          Patricia. All this is yours now.
          The library itself has been valued
          at a million dollars, and that was
          ten years ago.

                    PATRICIA
          But, she told me she was going to
          leave it to the city. The
          Quartermaine collection belongs to
          the university. The Shakespeare
          folio, the Gutenberg Bibles...
          What am I going to do with those?

                    LAWYER
          And then there's the money.

                    PATRICIA
          But Skipper and I have always had
          trusts.

                    LAWYER
          This is the real money. Your aunt
          was a very wealthy woman.

                    PATRICIA
          So they'd think I killed her for
          the money? The newspapers?

                    LAWYER
          Sells a lot of papers. I would
          suggest you go away after the
          funeral and come back when they've
          caught Andrew.

                    PATRICIA
          But Andrew didn't do it.

                    LAWYER
          That's for the police to..

The Maid enters.

                    MAID
          Excuse me, Mrs. Bevens. Mister
          Starkey is here.

                    PATRICIA
          It's all right. Tell him he can
          wait in the library.

                    LAWYER
          Someone from our office will take
          you to the inquest. If there's
          anything I can do in the meantime,
          let me know.

INT. LIBRARY - DAY

Jasper is pacing. Patricia enters.

                    JASPER
          Look, I've been up all night and I
          just don't believe Andrew did it.

                    PATRICIA
          Oh.

                    JASPER
          Do you think he did it?

                    PATRICIA
          I can't imagine anyone doing it.

                    JASPER
          But Andrew?

The PHONE RINGS, and without Andrew to answer, Patricia
picks it up herself.

                    PATRICIA
          Hello... Daisy! Oh, Daisy, oh,
          thank God you got my message!
          Well, I --
               (lowers her voice)
          -- can't really talk about it now,
          but something terrible has
          happened and I want to come stay
          with you for awhile...

Patricia has brightened and flowered since talking to
Daisy, and is no longer a wreck.

                    PATRICIA (CONT'D)
          Okay, I'll call you. Goodbye.

She puts down the phone and, with newfound confidence,
turns to Jasper.

INT. LIBRARY - NIGHT

Jasper falls asleep in the library. He has not left the
house since the murder.

INT. LIBRARY - MORNING

Patricia comes down and sees Jasper asleep on the couch.
She is in her bathrobe and looks adorable, disheveled
with her glasses.

Patricia finds one of the big Ronson lighters, and lights
a cigarette. She sits down and stares at Jasper while he
sleeps. She looks at what he's writing on the desk.

She reads his notes. Jasper wakes.

                    JASPER
          What's wrong? Who's here?
          (sitting up)
          Why, Miss Bevens, you're
          beautiful.

                    PATRICIA
          Did you write this?

                    JASPER
          It's that awful?

                    PATRICIA
          It's... it's totally great. You
          should publish this, it's very
          funny -- you should be a writer.

                    JASPER
          I am a writer.

                    PATRICIA
          But you should write books.

                    JASPER
          This ll a book.

                    PATRICIA
          But it should be published!

                    JASPER
          Well, that's a horse of a
          different color.

                    PATRICIA
          It will be.

                    JASPER
          You're in a good mood this
          morning, aren't you?

                    PATRICIA
             Maybe it's because
              I'm so rich.
              (bursting into)
             tears)
          Poor Aunt Susan.
                    (MORE)

                    PATRICIA (CONT'D)
          She takes me in when I've got no
          one -- I'm just a poor relation
          really -- from Baltimore. My
          parents both died, I've got no
          brothers or sisters - I'm sort of
          a cousin by the skin of my teeth --
          I thought she was leaving
          everything to Cal Tech -
          Boy, are they going to be
          surprised.

                    JASPER
          I guess she liked you. I don't
          blame her. Kiss me, you fool.

He pulls her gently toward him and before she has a
chance to start trembling, he kisses her tears away and
then licks them off her nose.

                    PATRICIA
          Kiss me, you fool, not my nose.

They kiss.

                    JASPER
          Where'd you learn this?

                    PATRICIA
          Why, am I awful?

                    JASPER
          Yes. I'm happy to say. You need
          help.

                    PATRICIA
          Help!

                    JASPER
          Didn't you learn anything when you
          were in college?

                    PATRICIA
          I went to finishing school and I
          wore glasses and was a wallflower.
                    (leans back, looking
                     at him)
          So teach me.

                    JASPER
          What about your husband?

                    PATRICIA
          Oh, him.

She gets up and begins to lunge for another cigarette.

                    JASPER
          Personal, eh?

                    PATRICIA
          Abysmally.

                    JASPER
          Come back, we'll start again. We
          have time. It's -- first you have
          to sit down...

She sits down warily.

                    PATRICIA
          Oh, no, my hands...

They're shaking. He takes her hands.

                    JASPER
          Then you close your eyes and
          pretend you're a big marshmallow
          bunny.

Patricia closes eyes, sags into his embrace

                    JASPER (CONT'D)
          And I'm the fox who's gonna eat
          you all up.

And, with that, he begins to kiss her and she lets out a
giggle which dissolves into a slow moan.

                    PATRICIA
          Gee. Rich and happy, both in one
          day.

A maid comes in and ruins everything.

INT. LIVING ROOM - LATER THAT DAY

A funereal-looking LAWYER is reading the will, then looks
at Patricia.

                    LAWYER
          Property in Malibu -- twenty-three
          twenty-eight Malibu Road. The
          ranch in San Ysidro, in addition
          to all stocks, bonds, and liquid
          assets. The library shall be
          transferred to the city as you
          requested.

                    PATRICIA
          Excuse me... how much money is
          liquid?

                    LAWYER
          You mean cash?

                    PATRICIA
          Yes.

                    LAWYER
          After taxes, I would estimate
          between three and four million.

EXT. CEMETERY - DAY

There is a small group of people around the grave, along
with a chaplain, who's reading the service.

ANGLE - PARKED CARS

We see the same Plymouth that was outside the
Quartermaine house.

EXT. ROAD TO SAN DIEGO - DAY

The top of Jasper's convertible is down. Skipper is
asleep in the back seat. Patricia and Jasper are gaily
blowing in the wind in front. Although Patricia is
dressed in her sober funeral clothes, she looks very
happy. She takes out a scarf and ties it around her head.

                    JASPER
               (trying not to be in
                love with her)
          What are you doing?

                    PATRICIA
          My hair...

Trying not to be in love with him.

                    JASPER
          Your hair's beautiful. What are
          you doing?

                    PATRICIA
          Okay...

She undoes her scarf and puts it back in her purse.

                    JASPER
Until Skipper wakes up, let's play
twenty questions. I'll ask you a
question and you can ask me one.

                    PATRICIA
What if he doesn't wake up?

                    JASPER
That's one. You've got nine left.
My turn. Why do play tennis if you
hate it?

                    PATRICIA
All the girls do it.

                    JASPER
How old are you?

                    PATRICIA
I'll be twenty-four. I was 19 when
I got married.

                    JASPER
How long were you married?

                    PATRICIA
That's... uh... personal.

                    JASPER
I'm sorry. young.
You go. You were so

                    PATRICIA
And dumb. Where'd you learn all
those hot moves?

                    JASPER
Like about the marshmallow? And
the fox?

                    PATRICIA
The boys I knew, they didn't know
anything. I mean, maybe they found
out -- but not from us. I came
from a small town and when Aunt
Susan sent the money for me to go
to finishing school, my parents
wanted to make sure it was one
where they didn't teach you
anything about life and you
couldn't possibly find out.
                  (MORE)

PATRICIA (CONT'D)
We learned to dance with other
girls and when we had these
socials with the boys from schools
around there, we had chaperons.
The only bad things we could think
to do was eat Hershey bars and
mashed potatoes.

                    JASPER

Together?

                    PATRICIA

We were hungry.

                    JASPER
So that's where you met... your
husband?

                    PATRICIA
The only reason he asked me to
dance was because of Daisy.

                    JASPER
The woman you're going to see?

                    PATRICIA
She was my best friend. And he was
her brother. I only danced with
him because he was tall.

                    JASPER
I take it this marriage was not...
a success.

                    PATRICIA
And you know, he got called back
from the honeymoon -- he and his
friends -- they were all shipped
to the islands. Where he was
killed. But I was pregnant. And
Aunt Susan invited me here. To
California. To be her companion.
Which was lucky because I need one
-- a companion -- myself. There I
was, nineteen, an orphan, pregnant
-- a complete idiot -- with
glasses. I was so happy she wrote
to me, I cried for the entire
train ride out. All I remember of
the United States is morning
sickness and Kleenex.

                    JASPER
          So have you seen Daisy since?

                    PATRICIA
          She's come to stay a couple of
          times. She couldn't believe I
          lived there. But she knew.

                    JASPER
          Knew what?

                    PATRICIA
          That Aunt Susan had changed her
          will.

                    JASPER
          She did?

                    PATRICIA

Yes. Funny, isn't it? Aunt Susan told her. The last time
she was here, a month ago, she said not to worry about
me, that she was leaving me everything.

                    JASPER
          Why?

                    PATRICIA
          I think Daisy was worried about me
          ... I don't know... Anyway, she
          made Daisy promise not to tell me.
          Or anyone. Aunt Susan liked to be
          sneaky. How'd you get Aunt Susan
          to let you use the library? She
          won't let people from Hollywood
          in.

                    JASPER
          I wrote the library a fan letter.

                    PATRICIA
          You're so cute.

EXT. BEACH - DAY

They are sitting on the beach with Skipper, having a
picnic -- watercress sandwiches, lemonade, and gin.

                    PATRICIA
          This stuff tastes horrible.

                         JASPER
          Did you hear the one about the guy
          who dies, and he's at the pearly
          gates, and Saint Peter says,
          'Where you from?,' and he says
          'Los Angeles,' and Saint Peter
          says, 'Well, you can come in, but
          I don't think you're going to like
          it.'

                         PATRICIA
          Aunt Susan always said that
          Pasadena wasn't really part of Los
          Angeles. She thought Pasadena and
          Santa Barbara were vacation spots
          for respectable people from good
          families and that Los Angeles and
          Hollywood were just too bad.

                         JASPER
          Like me.

                         PATRICIA
          Actually, she liked you. But you
          do work in the movies.

                         JASPER
          A lot of people work in the
          movies. Look at William Faulkner.

                         PATRICIA
          Who's William Faulkner?

Skipper approaches them carrying a sand dollar.

                         SKIPPER
              (handing shell to
               Jasper)
          Daddy?

                         PATRICIA
          Daddy's gone, darling.

                         JASPER
          Hubba hubba.

EXT. HIGHWAY - DAY

They are back on the road, driving south. Skipper is in
the back, humming to himself. Patricia sits close to
Jasper this time.

                    JASPER
          Tell me again what you did that
          day.

                    PATRICIA
          Well, I did what I always do. I
          went upstairs, changed into my
          bathing suit, got my robe, and
          went down to the pool. Four
          o'clock. I always go swimming at
          four o'clock. Except Sundays.

                    JASPER
          So you're at the pool and you see
          your aunt. And she was all right.

                    PATRICIA
          She was asleep. She's old, she
          takes... took naps. She was
          reading a magazine, this week's,
          and she'd been drinking iced tea.

                    JASPER
          Wait a second. You said the only
          reason Andrew came down to the
          pool was to bring her iced tea.

                    PATRICIA
          That's right. But she already had
          iced tea.

                    JASPER
          So you get down to the pool and
          then what do you do? Exactly?

                    PATRICIA
          I take my robe off and dive in.

                    JASPER
          Where are your glasses?

                    PATRICIA
          I don't swim with my glasses!
          They're at the edge of the pool.

She laughs.

                    JASPER
            Let me see.

Patricia hands him her glasses.

Jasper puts the glasses to his eyes. They are so strong
that the shock makes Jasper jerk backwards and almost
swerve the car into an accident.

He gulps and looks pale when he gets the car back under
control. He's too shaken to even be a smart ass for once.

Patricia primly puts her glasses back on.

                    PATRICIA
          I'm blind as a bat. Legally blind,
          it's called.

                    JASPER
          When you don't have your glasses
          on, what can you see?

                    PATRICIA
          Well, anything beyond a three-foot
          radius is a blur.

                    JASPER
          Well, how did you know it was
          Andrew?

                    PATRICIA
          It had to be Andrew. I could tell
          by the colors. Light hair, white
          jacket, and white pants. He was
          coming down to bring her iced tea.
          I can tell who a person is by
          colors and what time it is.
          And, anyway, I always wear my
          glasses and my eyesight's perfect.
          Except when I'm not wearing them.

Skipper leans up against the front seat.

                    SKIPPER
          Hubba hubba.

EXT. LA JOLLA - DAY

They are driving down a dusty road. Avocado trees in rows
line both sides of the driveway. It's an avocado ranch in
La Jolla, slightly inland. There's something untended and
overgrown about this place. Since the war, it's been hard
to find men to work there.

The car pulls up to a large, rambling, ranch/farm-type
two-story house, which also needs paint and repairs.

On the front porch, waving happily, is a young woman,
DAISY, with her five-year-old daughter, AMANDA, a little
girl with pink ribbons on her braids. She's a perfect
foil for Skipper in his sailor suit. Adorable. If they
only got along picturesquely, they would be surefire
models for sentimental greeting cards.

But Patricia and Daisy get along fine. The friendship
between these two young women is solid, and has been
since they were fourteen.

                    DAISY
          Patricia!

She races down the creaking steps and throws her arms
around Patricia, who is equally overjoyed to see Daisy.

                    PATRICIA
          Daze! good! you. At last! Oh, you
          look so It's so wonderful to see
          you.

                    DAISY
          Oh, I wanted to see you so often,
          but, with no one here, I can't
          leave...

                    PATRICIA
          It's been so long. Look at Amanda,
          how big she is. She's going to
          have to marry a tall man!

                    DAISY
               (turning to Jasper)
            Hello, I'm Daisy
            Bowers.

                    JASPER
          I'm --

                    PATRICIA
          Daisy, this is Mister Starkey.
          He's in the movies and knows
          people in the black market.

                    JASPER
               (protesting)
            Patricia...

                    DAISY
          Can you get stockings? Nylons? My
          husband's coming back any day and
          my legs are a mess.

She stands back, and her legs are not a mess.

                    JASPER
          What size?

                    DAISY
          Six. Tan, if I have a choice.

                    JASPER
              (locks it into his
               memory)
          Six-tan.

                    PATRICIA
          Mister Starkey is from Los
          Angeles.

She says this as though Los Angeles were about as unknown
and improbable as Tibet.

The kids have burst into tears and are tugging apart a
toy. Patricia is attempting to deal with the children for
the first time in her life, and not succeeding. Daisy
runs into the fray.

Jasper looks innocently at this sweet domestic upheaval
and, when he walks, we notice once again that he has a
limp.

Jasper removes a business card from his wallet and gives
it to Patricia.

                    JASPER
          My office number is here, and my
          home number is on the back.

                    DAISY
          There's plenty of room if you'd
          care to stay, Mister Starkey.

                    JASPER
          Jasper, please. I'd like to, but I
          have an early appointment.
          (to Patricia) Tell Skipper hubba
          hubba.

Jasper gets in his car, waves goodbye and drives off.

EXT. DAISY'S HOUSE (LA JOLLA) - SOMEONE'S POV - NIGHT

FROM a hill, overlooking Daisy's backyard. The ANGLE
WIDENS to include the old Plymouth that was spying in
Pasadena. It gives off the same eerie feeling. Danger
seems imminent.

EXT. DAISY'S HOUSE - NIGHT

Daisy and Patricia are sitting on the front porch swing
in comfort and peace. Patricia has removed her glasses
and laid them down on the floor beside the swing. The two
women are drinking beer from cans.

                    DAISY
               (picking up the
                glasses and
                squinting through
                them)
          I forgot how blind you were.

                    PATRICIA
          Everybody thought I was clumsy,
          remember? Even my nanny.

                    DAISY
          Wasn't it Mrs. Bowen who finally
          figured it out?

                    PATRICIA
          She took me to the school nurse,
          and then right out of the building
          to the eye doctor. And the next
          thing I knew, I started getting
          A's in math. I could read the
          blackboard.

Daisy is about to say something. Patricia holds up her
hand.

                    PATRICIA (CONT'D)
          Shhhhh.

There is a moment when they both listen. Patricia puts
her glasses on, the better to listen and concentrate.

                    PATRICIA (CONT'D)
          I thought I heard Skipper.

                    DAISY
          It was probably the cats.

                    PATRICIA
          Are you sure? Maybe I worry about
          him too much. If anything happened
          to him, there'd be no one.

                    DAISY
          Was it hard for you after Mark --

                    PATRICIA
          It was awful. I had to wear black
          for a year. And I was pregnant.
          I thought the baby was going to
          have to wear black diapers. You
          know how it is in Pasadena. But,
          thank God, Aunt Susan's so... was
          so eccentric.

                    DAISY
          It must have been horrible

Patricia just shakes her head.

                    DAISY (CONT'D)
          Change the subject, Patricia.

                    PATRICIA
               (obliges)
          When is Richard coming home?

                    DAISY
          I don't know. He's in the
          Philippines, and there's some
          trouble. They've got all these
          ships just waiting in the harbor,
          and they're not letting anyone on
          them. It's ironic, isn't it? I
          mean, the goddamn war is over...

                    PATRICIA
          Yes, Daisy, the war _is_ over.

                    DAISY
          I haven't seen Richard in three
          years. The whole ranch is
          overgrown with weeds. I can't get
          any help; everyone went to work in
          the plants or overseas...

                    PATRICIA
          Well, he's not going to blame you
          for that. He'll just be glad to be
          home and see you and Amanda.

                         DAISY
              Well, how would you feel if Mark
              was coming home?

                         PATRICIA
              Of course, I'd be glad. But we
              barely knew each other, and then
              he went to sea. I can hardly
              remember him.

                         DAISY
              I can.

                         PATRICIA
              I'm sorry, Daisy.

EXT. SAN GABRIEL MOUNTAINS - CLIFFSIDE - DAY

There's a crane and a tow truck, a couple of police cars,
the Police Chief, and the Ace Detective. They are in the
process of hauling a badly mashed and mangled car from
the ravine.

Jasper's convertible pulls up to the dusty roadside. He
parks and gets out, then comes over to look. He stands
there as the car is towed up.

A black police "meat wagon" is parked beside the road.

The Police Chief walks Jasper over to the meat wagon,
opens the door, and we see a canvas shroud. The Police
Chief pulls back part of the canvas. Jasper looks at it
for a brief moment, then turns away with an awful
expression.

The two men walk back toward the car.

To a uniformed COP:

                         POLICE CHIEF
              Show him.

The Cop opens the trunk of the police car and points.

                         COP
              That's the knife we think he
              killed the old…Mrs. Quartermaine
              with...
                   (points to corpse)
              And we don't know for sure exactly
              how much, but we think he must
              have drunk about a pint of Mrs.
              Quartermaine's Canadian whiskey.

He shows Jasper a shard of glass with the label still on
it.

                    JASPER
          Jesus Christ.

EXT. ROADSIDE CAFE - DAY

Jasper's car is pulled up outside. This is a dusty little
one-horse diner near where the car was found. Jasper is
feeding quarters into a pay phone outside.

                              INTERCUT WITH:

EXT. FARMHOUSE - DAY

Rural San Diego County. Avocado and orange groves
surround the house and modest barn.

INT.FARMHOUSE KITCHEN -

Patricia on the phone. In the b.g. Skipper and a girl his
age chase each other around the table, while DAISY, the
girl's mother (Patricia's sister-in-law) listens.

                    PATRICIA
          Drunk? Andrew? Jasper, that's
          impossible. Andrew wasn't supposed
          to drink.

                    JASPER
          You can say that again.

                    PATRICIA
          I mean, he can't. It's some
          medical thing. Ask our doctor,
          Doctor Larson. It was something
          like an allergy.

                    JASPER
          What's all that racket?

                    PATRICIA
          Oh, the kids. They're waiting. A
          birthday party, you know, in town.

                    JASPER
          I'm going to find out about
          Andrew. If I find out anything?

                    PATRICIA
          We should be back here about five.

                    JASPER
          Is it too soon to miss you?

                    PATRICIA
          I've missed you for hours.

The answer leaves him somewhat speechless.

                    JASPER
              I'll call you.

Jasper leaves the phone booth and gets into his car. We
see a sign reading: Los Angeles 35 miles.

EXT. STREET (LA JOLLA) - DAY

A station wagon carrying Patricia, Daisy, and the two
kids, dressed for a birthday party, stops in front of a
large house. Both kids carry presents as they get out of
the car. We watch Daisy take them to the front door where
they wave goodbye to Patricia. The front door closes
behind them.

Daisy returns to the car, gets in, and they drive away.

                    DAISY
              Thank God for other children's
              birthdays. We've got three hours
              all to ourselves.

EXT. MEDICAL BUILDING (PASADENA) - DAY

Jasper pulls up. We see very fancy cars in the lot.

INT. MEDICAL BUILDING - DAY

                    RECEPTIONIST
              The doctor won't see anyone
              without an appointment.

                    JASPER
              I'll make one. Jasper Starkey,
              Vice-President of Warner Bros.
              Referred by Susan Quartermaine.
              Today anytime.

He sits down. She can do nothing. The big clock behind
her indicates 3:30.

A few dignified and patronizing older patients glance at him without blinking. He waits.

EXT. MOVIE THEATRE (LA JOLLA) - DAY

Daisy and Patricia come out and go to the car.

EXT. BIRTHDAY PARTY HOUSE - DAY

Daisy parks the as she talks to grows animated lurches towards the car.

car and goes to the front door. We watch the birthday mother. The conversation Daisy turns around, looking ashen, and the car. Patricia starts to get out of

                         PATRICIA
              Daisy?

INT. MEDICAL BUILDING - DOCTOR'S OFFICE - DAY

The clock now indicates 5:30. The room is empty save for Jasper, who is still waiting.

                         RECEPTIONIST
                   (to Jasper) You can
                   go in now.

INT. DOCTOR'S STUDY - DAY

DOCTOR LARSON sits behind the desk. He's reading a chart. Jasper enters.

                         DR. LARSON
              Mister Starkey... an acquaintance
              of Mrs. Bevens?

Doctor Larson can't believe someone as un-Pasadena as Jasper is actually a friend of Patricia Bevens.

                         JASPER
              I've been doing research at the
              library.

                         DR. LARSON
              Well, what seems to be the
              trouble?

                    JASPER
          Trouble? Oh, no, no, no, I'm fine.
          It's Mrs. Quartermaine's... it's
          Andrew. The police found him and
          his car at the bottom of a cliff.
          He'd been dead four days. Anyway,
          they figure he killed her and they
          found the knife, too. And
          apparently he'd been drinking.

                    DR. LARSON
          Drinking? Not possible.

                    JASPER
          That's what Patricia Bevens
          thought. She said you would know.

                    DR. LARSON
          I've been Andrew's doctor for
          twenty years. Andrew had a toxic
          reaction to any form of alcohol.
          Half an ounce and he's unconscious
          for twelve hours.

INT. RECEPTION AREA

Jasper is leaving. The Receptionist is gone.

EXT. PARKING LOT

Jasper has started his car. Doctor Larson comes rushing
out of the building, waving his arms to Jasper. Jasper
sees him.

INT. DOCTOR LARSON'S STUDY

Jasper is on the phone.

                    JASPER
          Incredible. I'm on my way.

Jasper hangs up. He turns to Doctor Larson.

                    JASPER (CONT'D)
          I've got to go back to La Jolla.
          Somebody kidnapped Skipper.

He gets to the door, then turns back.

                    JASPER (CONT'D)
          Do you have any of those pills?
          You know, those pills they take to
          stay up?

                    DR. LARSON
          Benzadrine.

EXT. PARKING LOT

As he gets into his car, he pops one of the pills into
his mouth. He waits a moment.

                    JASPER
          Now they got her kid. Why don't
          they leave her alone?

INT. HOUSE (LA JOLLA} - BIRTHDAY PARTY - DAY

Two plain-clothes DETECTIVES are asking questions.
THROUGH a window we can see Uniformed Officers waiting
outside. The birthday mother, GLORIA, is in tears. Daisy
is angry and Patricia is the calmest one of all, trying
to be helpful to Gloria.

                    GLORIA
               (in tears}
          But, he said... he was Amanda's
          father. He was in a Navy uniform.
          You called me!

                    DAISY
          No, I didn't. I didn't.

                    GLORIA
          You did. You did. You said...
          someone said... it was a surprise.

                    PATRICIA
               (to Gloria)
          Amanda's father is in the Army.

                    DETECTIVE #!
          Do you remember the car?

                    GLORIA
          Car? I had all these kids leaving
          at once with mothers and fathers
          ... There's ice cream all over
          everything... Daisy, I didn't
          know. I'm sorry.

                    DAISY
          Naval uniform! You knew he was in
          the Army!

                    DETECTIVE #1
          Well, do you remember what he
          looked like?

                    GLORIA
          He was handsome and polite. And he
          acted like a father.

                    DETECTIVE #2
          Well, if it's a kidnapping.

                    DAISY
          Well, of course it's a kidnapping!
          Two children are gone!

The PHONE RINGS. A MAID, was has answered it, comes into
the room.

                    MAID
          Mrs. Bowers?

                    DAISY
          For me? But, who --

                    DETECTIVE #1
          Is there an extension?

He is shown out of the room.

                    DAISY
               (on phone)
          Hello?

                    MAIL VOICE (V.O.)
               (filtered)
          I've got the kids. Get fifty
          thousand dollars. You'll hear from
          me.

BAM. He hangs up.

                    DAISY
               (looks up from dead
                phone)
          Oh, God.

                    PATRICIA
          Skipper?

                         DAISY
          Oh, God.

The Detective enters.

                         DETECTIVE #1
                    (to Daisy)
          Do you have that kind of money?

                         DAISY
          No.

                         PATRICIA
          I do.

INT. JASPER'S CAR - NIGHT

Jasper is leaning satanically over the steering wheel,
going as fast as he can.

He's a menace on the highway. TRUCKS HONK at his slippery
style. He's talking to himself, smoking two cigarettes at
a time.

                         JASPER
          Boy, I'd like to catch this son of
          a bitch... break both his arms.
          That poor kid, what kind of a
          bastard would do something like
          that? Well, this guy's got me to
          reckon with now. Something he
          didn't count on. Poor defenseless
          women...

EXT. HIGHWAY - ROAD-SIGN - NIGHT "SAN DIEGO -- CITY
LIMITS"

                                        BACK TO SCENE

Jasper is singing "Clementine" at the top of his voice.

EXT. DAISY'S HOUSE - DAWN

Jasper, a shadow of his former self, shakily gets out of
his car. He has been driving for eleven hours, and his
knees nearly buckle under him.

He takes out the second pill, looks at it for a moment,
then pops it.

He swaggers up to the front door. No one would ever want
to see him, he knows, in his present condition. But this
is unimportant to him now.

Lurking in the shadows is a La Jolla cop named SERGEANT
BRIGGS. He is a fifty-year-old man who is determined to
become a hero before all the vets come back with Silver
Stars. This case is his last chance. He has a gun.

                    BRIGGS
          Hold it right there, fella.

                    JASPER
          It's all right. I'm a friend of
          the family. Just drove down from
          L.A. What's the latest?

                    BRIGGS
          (eternally suspicious) L.A., huh?
          Let's see your identification.

Jasper talks as he hands over his i.d. Briggs takes the
whole wallet.

                    JASPER
          Look, I know about the kidnapping.
          Is there a note? Have you heard
          anything yet? How's Patricia? I
          mean, Mrs. Bevens? That's my
          studio pass, my Writer's Guild
          card, license, and --
                    (turns to house and
                     yells)
          Patricia!

We see an upstairs WINDOW RUSTLE and open.

                    PATRICIA
          (looks out)
          Jasper... Come in! I'll be right
          down.

Jasper dashes into the house, followed by Briggs still
clutching Jasper's papers.

INT. DAISY'S HOUSE - LIVING ROOM - DAY

Daisy has been dozing on the couch. Two FBI AGENTS are
responsible for all the smoke hanging in the room, and
the full ashtrays. The phone is the focal point of this
room.

As Patricia comes down the stairs.

                    JASPER
               (to Patricia)
     I just drove all night, but I feel
     fine. Great. How are you? Look
     great. Fresh as a daisy. Daisy
     doesn't look half as fresh. Hey,
     everything's going to be all
     right.

                    PATRICIA
     What's the matter with you?

                    JASPER
     Nothing's the matter with me. I'm
     awake, that's the important thing.
     And I'm going to stay awake until
     this thing's over. What about
     Skipper? Heard anything? How's
     Amanda?

                    PATRICIA
     They want fifty thousand dollars,
     and the bank will have it this
     morning.

                    JASPER
     Great. I'll drive you over. Who're
     these guys?

                    PATRICIA
     These gentlemen are from the
     F.B.I.

The two FBI guys rise to their feet, tired but polite.

                    JASPER
     How do you do. I'm Jasper Lido.
     F.B.I., huh? You guys get here
     quick.

                    AGENT MORRISON (FBI)
     I'm Special Agent Morrison. This
     is Special Agent Shawn. It's a
     waiting game, I'm afraid.

                    DAISY
     Are you hungry?

                    JASPER
     Oh, no.

                    PATRICIA
     Did you stop on the way?

                    JASPER
          Just for gas. How long do we have
          to wait? Let's do something.
          What's the next step?

Daisy picks up a cigarette. Jasper thrusts a lighter at
her so quickly she drops the cigarette. He reaches down
for the cigarette, and, in the process, almost knocks
over an ashtray stand. The FBI Agents suddenly become
more interested in this man.

                    AGENT MORRISON
          Mrs. Bevens called you about the
          kidnapping?

                    JASPER
          Right. Right. I was at the
          doctor's office. Oh, Patricia...
          Mrs. Bevens... you were right.
          Andrew didn't drink. In fact, it
          was impossible for him to drink.
          He couldn't have done it. He had
          that thing...
                    (looks to the FBI
                     guys for help; they
                     have no idea what
                     he's talking about)
          What's it called when you can't
          drink? I forgot the term. It
          starts with... It's a medical
          word... Anyway, it changed
          everything --

                    DAISY
          Mister Starkey, will you shut up?

                    JASPER
          I can't. Yes, I can. I've shut up.

                    DAISY
          I'm sorry. I'm just not myself.

                    JASPER
          Neither am I. Is anybody hungry?
          I'll go and make something. Is
          anybody hungry?

No one is, obviously. Jasper lets the moment pass.

                    JASPER (CONT'D)
          I'll just sit down.

After a moment, Jasper has to start talking again.

                    JASPER (CONT'D)
          How did this happen? Could
          somebody tell me?

                    PATRICIA
          We left Skipper and Amanda at a
          birthday party, and a woman called
          Mrs. Jameson, said she was Daisy,
          and that her husband was going to
          pick up the kids... and then some
          guy in a Navy uniform.

                    AGENT SHAWN
          Officer's uniform.

                    PATRICIA
          That's right. A Navy officer's
          uniform. He said he was the
          father, so she thought it was all
          right --
                    (starts to cry)
          -- and then he put them in a car
          and drove away.

Jasper gets up and puts his arms around her. She cries
just a tiny bit on his shoulder.

                    JASPER
          How did he know those kids would
          be there? Or that Mrs. Jameson
          wouldn't know he wasn't your
          husband? This guy knew a lot and
          what kind of kidnapper would take
          little kids? Isn't that asking for
          trouble?

                    AGENT MORRISON
          A lot of times their wives or girl
          friends take care of the kids.
          Sometimes the kids end up none the
          worse. It's like a game to them.

                    DAISY
          You think?

                    AGENT MORRISON
          See it all the time.

                    PATRICIA
          But, they're babies.

                    AGENT MORRISON
          You're lucky.

                    JASPER
          A five-year-old kid isn't a very
          good witness. Patricia, I must
          have a private word with you.

INT. DAISY'S KITCHEN - DAY

Jasper has calmed down somewhat, and he and Patricia are
talking.

                    JASPER
          Look, I've been thinking about
          this thing, and it's just like a
          plot. -- Somebody kills your aunt,
          tries to make it look like Andrew
          dit it, kills Andrew - and you
          inherit all her money... and then
          your child is kidnapped. Don't you
          see?

                    PATRICIA
          See what?

                    JASPER
          Now you have money for the ransom.
          It's all part of some chain --
          And he knows too much about you,
          your family. It has to be someone
          you know.

Before Patricia can answer, Daisy enters holding a blue
velvet box.

                    DAISY
          Patricia... I want you to have
          this... sell them for my half of
          the ransom.

                    PATRICIA
               (opening box)
          But you don't have to -- My God,
          these are lovely. Daisy, not this!

Jasper looks inside and sees the same diamond/emerald
necklace and earring set we saw in the first scene in the
jewelry store on Hollywood Boulevard.

                    JASPER
          May I?

Looks more closely at the set.

                    DAISY
          They were Richard's grandmother's.

For the first time, he looks at Daisy askance. He is
suspicious, as well he should be.

                    PATRICIA
          I won't let you. I have so much.

                    DAISY
          Please.

                    PATRICIA
          No. Absolutely no.

                    DAISY
          Thank you. God bless you.

INT. BANK OFFICE - DAY

Patricia and Jasper and a BANK EXECUTIVE are there, as
well as the Pasadena Lawyer who oversees the Quartermaine
affairs. He's come down to supervise anything he can.
Agent Morrison is there, too. The Bank Executive, under
the watchful eye of the Lawyer, is counting the money and
stuffing it into a valise. It's a lot of money, even now.

                    PATRICIA
          Is this money marked?

The Bank Executive is halfway done and stops.

                    LAWYER
          Mrs. Bevens, it's fifty thousand
          dollars.

                    PATRICIA
          I want my son back and I want
          unmarked money. If you insist on
          giving me this money, I'll go to
          the bank across the street and
          exchange it.

                    JASPER
              (to the Lawyer) Is
          the money marked?

                    LAWYER
          The money's not marked.

                    PATRICIA
          You promise?

                    LAWYER
          I give you my word.

EXT. ROAD TO DAISY'S HOUSE - DAY

Jasper and Patricia drive into the ranch. They are
followed by the FBI car and Lawyer. It seems they are
always to be followed.

EXT. DAISY'S HOUSE - DAY

Daisy is standing on the porch looking drawn. The two FBI
guys are in the shadows. They are very obvious.

                    PATRICIA
          Nothing?

Daisy shakes her head.

                    DAISY
          Did you get it?

The Lawyer comes up the walk carrying the valise.

INT. DAISY'S LIVING ROOM - DAY

The two FBI guys, Daisy, Patricia, Jasper, the Lawyer,
and Sergeant Briggs are dying of heat prostration in the
living room where a couple of flies circle in the one
hundred degree heat. Everybody has wilted except Jasper,
who will never wilt.

                    DAISY
          I can't stand these clothes. I've
          got to change.

She catches Patricia's eye meaningfully and indicates
upstairs.

                    PATRICIA
          Oh, God, yes.

Both women go upstairs.

The FBI Agents stare at the flies in silence as they
leave.

INT. DAISY'S BEDROOM - DAY

Daisy leads Patricia into the bedroom and shuts the door.

She opens a dresser drawer and takes out an envelope.

                    DAISY
          Paco found this on the windshield
          of the station wagon.

Patricia opens the envelope and reads the note.

                    PATRICIA
          Rosarito Beach?

Patricia looks at Daisy.

                    DAISY
          It's across the border. Below
          Tijuana.

                    PATRICIA
          Then we'll go. No police.

                    DAISY
          You're right.

                    PATRICIA
          Just don't say anything. I'll
          handle this.

INT. LIVING ROOM - DAY

As it was a few minutes ago. Unbearable. A dry oven. It's
too hot to complain, or even talk. But none of this
affects Jasper, who, still reeling from the two bennies,
has three cigarettes and four conversations going.

                    JASPER
          I did an F.B.I. picture once.
          Well, I didn't write the whole
          thing, they took me off it to do a
          Western. Got story credit, though.
          Maybe you saw it. It was called
          ... actually, I called it... but
          they changed my title and I don't
          remember what they called it.

Sergeant Briggs catches a fly in his fist.

                    JASPER (CONT'D)
          Very good. You have good reflexes.
          That must be important in your
          work. Do you get much crime here
          in La Jolla?

Briggs looks at him, appalled. At that moment, Patricia
and Daisy descend the stairs. Patricia stops at the
landing. Daisy stands behind her. Patricia waits until
everyone's attention has turned to her.

                    PATRICIA
          I want you all to leave.

This wakes up the room.

                    PATRICIA (CONT'D)
          Mrs. Bowers and I have decided we
          want to handle this in our own
          way. We have the money and we what
          to do.

                    AGENT MORRISON
          Ma'am, our experience in these
          matters is that --

                    PATRICIA
          We don't want to discuss it. Will
          you all please go?

They get up and head for the door.

                    JASPER
          Wait a minute. You guys aren't
          going to go! There's a crime here.
          She's hysterical. Don't listen to
          her. F.B.I... this is kidnapping!

                    AGENT MORRISON
          Mister Starkey, is it? Our policy
          is that we will not get involved
          in a case without the cooperation
          of the victims. When the children
          are returned, we'll pursue the
          investigation and try to apprehend
          the kidnappers and recover the
          money. But right now our hands are
          tied.
                    (to Patricia)
          If you change your mind, Mrs.
          Bevens, give us a call.

Sergeant Briggs gets up, too. Jasper walks with them to
the door and outside.

EXT. DAISY'S HOUSE - DAY

The FBI Agents get into their car. Jasper catches up to
Briggs.

                    JASPER
          Briggs, can't you do anything?

                    BRIGGS
          Mister, they're going to give the
          money to the kidnapper, and
          they're either going to get their
          kids back, or not.

                    JASPER
          Not?

                    BRIGGS
          Not. It happens that way, too.
          What do you want me to do, Mister
          Starkey?

                    JASPER
          Follow them.

                    BRIGGS
          In this?

He indicates the bright black and white police car.
Briggs shrugs, gets in the car, and drives away. Jasper
turns back to the house.

Patricia and Daisy are on the front porch, waiting,
dressed for a journey. Patricia carries the valise with
the money.

The three of them watch the cars disappear.

                    DAISY
          I'll wait in the car.

She heads off toward the station wagon.

                    JASPER
          Where are you going?

She hands him the note. Jasper reads it.

                    JASPER (CONT'D)
          I won't follow you. I'll just be
          at the hotel in Rosarito. If
          anything happens, you'll want me
          there. You don't have anyone else.

                    PATRICIA
          There's Daisy.

He's about to question her on that, but, before he can,
she runs past him and gets in the car with Daisy.

They drive off. Jasper stares after them.

EXT. HIGHWAY - AERIAL SHOT - DAY

Daisy's station wagon heading south along the ocean.
Jasper's Cadillac follows at a considerable distance.

EXT. GAS STATION - DAY

Daisy and Patricia are watching a MECHANIC gingerly
remove the radiator cap.

He leaps back as a geyser of steaming water erupts from
the radiator.

                    MECHANIC
          I'll let it cool off for awhile.

Patricia nods, looks up, and sees Jasper's car drive by.

                    DAISY
          Want some pop?

Patricia walks over to the pop cooler and accepts a Coke
and a straw from Daisy.

                    PATRICIA
          Thanks. I'll drive the rest of the
          way.

                    DAISY
          I feel all right...

                    PATRICIA
          I'm sure you do, but you didn't
          notice the goddam temperature
          gauge. Oh, I don't know why I'm
          saying these things... Forget it.
          I'm sorry, Daze. It's the heat and
          everything.

Daisy nods, and they head back to the car.

INT. STATION WAGON - DAY

Patricia is driving. She notices Jasper's car getting gas
at a filling station. She continues driving.

EXT. ROAD - DAY (LATER)

To the right, gentle green slopes working their way to
the ocean. To the left, it's poor, dry, and monotonous:
the desert.

EXT. JASPER'S CAR - JASPER - DAY

Jasper is listening to the car RADIO. It's a SAN DIEGO
STATION talking about the end of the war.

                         RADIO NEWS ANNOUNCER (V.O.)
                ... Reports that Army troops in
                Manila have rioted in efforts to
                board waiting ships were denied by
                the Secretary of the Army...

EXT. ROSARITA BEACH HOTEL - DAY

As it used to be: a smaller, den-of-iniquity Mexican
version of the Hotel Del Coronado. It's right on the
beach with a pool overlooking the ocean with a patio

for drinks. There are three huge tile bars with mariachi
bands, a beamed ceiling, cool, dark tile floors.

A lot of men in uniform and girls with ruffled dresses
are celebrating the end of the war. The place is bustling
and happy. Our two women are nervous and intense.

They walk up to the registration desk and ignore the good-
natured spirit of the place. They don't see Jasper at the
adjacent dark bar, but he sees them.

JASPER'S POV

He watches Patricia and Daisy register. A band is play
ing Mexican versions of American songs, drowning out the
voices of the desk clerk, Daisy and Patricia.

INT. HOTEL ROOM - DAY

Daisy and Patricia enter and put down their bags. The
room is empty and sad.

                         DAISY
                I've run out of cigarettes.

                         PATRICIA
                I think they sell them downstairs.

                    DAISY
          You need anything?

                    PATRICIA
          I'll be all right.

Daisy leaves and shuts the door quietly behind her.

Patricia sits down on the bed and removes her glasses and
then begins to sob, first sitting up and then face-down
on the bed.

EXT. HALLWAY OUTSIDE PATRICIA'S ROOM - DAY

Jasper is standing outside and hears PATRICIA'S SOBS.
Then he knocks.

                    JASPER
          Are you okay?

Patricia opens the door, her eyes red from crying.

                    PATRICIA
          Well, no.

                    JASPER
          How about coming downstairs? Maybe
          a drink will help.

                    PATRICIA
          Help? Nothing will help. Not until
          I have Skipper back.

                    JASPER
          Well, wash your face and come down
          anyway. You can watch me drink.

                    PATRICIA
          Maybe some coffee.

INT. HOTEL LOBBY - DAY

Jasper is on long distance, shouting to Hollywood.

                    JASPER
               (into phone)
          No, we can't work down here...
          Monte, I don't know when I'll be
          back... No, I can't tell you what
          ... Look, why is this bothering
          you? What's the big deal?...
          They've never sued a writer yet.
                    (MORE)

                    JASPER (CONT'D)
          It's just something they say.
          I'll call you tomorrow.

Patricia is standing in back of him, listening.

                    PATRICIA
          Jasper? Why are you here?

                    JASPER
          It's what you do when you love
          somebody.

She looks at him blankly. He tries again.

                    JASPER (CONT'D)
          Me. You.

                    PATRICIA
          Oh, Jasper. I knew this would
          happen. I mean I wanted it to
          happen... I guess it's too late
          now.

                    JASPER
          Too late?

                    PATRICIA
          To be sensible.

She smiles through her desperation and almost laughs, if
she could laugh. Jason takes her in his arms.

                    JASPER
          Listen, it's going to be okay. You
          have the money, we'll hear from
          them soon, and it and the world
          will be peaceful.

                    PATRICIA
          Can we get something to eat?

INT. ROSARITA DINING ROOM - DAY

They're sitting there with lots of uneaten food in front
of them.

A hotel EMPLOYEE approaches.

                    BELLBOY {EMPLOYEE)
          Senora?

                    PATRICIA
          Yes?

He hands her a note. She gives him a tip. He leaves. She opens the note, Jasper reads it over her shoulder.

                    JASPER
          I'll go.

Daisy appears.

                    PATRICIA
          I'll go.

                    JASPER
          I'll go with you.

                    PATRICIA
          It says only one of the ladies...

                    JASPER
          I'll follow you.

                    DAISY
          No!

They turn to her.

                    DAISY (CONT'D)
          I want to do what the note says.

                    PATRICIA
          Daisy's right.

EXT. HOTEL - DAY

Patricia is getting into the car, Jasper and Daisy watch her.

                    DAISY
               (to Jasper)
          I want to wait in my room.

She flees inside.

EXT. HIGHWAY - DAY

Patricia is heading south toward Ensenada. She stops at an intersection to make a left hand turn up a dirt road leading to the dry hills. Patricia's car stands out in the solitary landscape; everything looks dangerous -- so lonely and desperate.

EXT. BURNT-OUT CHURCH - DAY

Patricia arrives. One lone goat and five chickens are the only visible life. The adobe shell has no door on its hinges, and no windows. She parks.

She gets out of the car. The silence of no motor, just the CHICKENS and the RUSTY BELL on the GOAT's neck, makes things oppressively strange.

Patricia reaches into the car and gets out the valise. She stands there and waits.

A terrible CRY freezes her for a moment, then she turns.

ANGLE - CHURCH

A braying BURRO, the source of the CRY, walks out from behind the wall. Atop the burro are Skipper and Amanda, flushed with laughter. They couldn't be happier. They are wearing sombreros, zapatas, and gorging themselves on lollipops.

There's a Mexican peasant standing in the church doorway shadows, dressed wearing a sombrero, white pants, and a white shirt.

Patricia walks toward him with the valise.

LOUD ENGINE NOISE.

EXT. DIRT ROAD - DAY

Jasper's Cadillac shoots out toward the clearing, heading straight for the Mexican.

PATRICIA Drops the valise.

MEXICAN MAN

Starts to go for the suitcase, the Cadillac bearing down on him. He can't make it. He turns and dashes toward the church.

CADILLAC

SKIDS to a halt between the church and the suitcase.

CHURCH

The man, now on a horse, leaps over a crumpled wall and
gallops off into the desert, dodging the large boulders
and cacti.

CADILLAC

Heads for the desert and then stops. There's no road and
it would be impossible.

JASPER

Climbs out of the Cadillac and runs back to where
Patricia is holding the burro that the children are on.
He stops to pick up the valise. The children are waving
at the man on the horse.

                    SKIPPER
          Goodbye, Daddy. <u>Adios</u>.

                    AMANDA
          He let us ride the burro. And I
          got to stay up all night. But I
          feel asleep.

Jasper hugs everyone in sight.

                    JASPER
          We got 'em!!
               (waving the valise)
          And the money, too! We got 'um!!
          Yess sirreee-bob, we got 'um.

There is much hugging and squealing between Patricia and
the children, Patricia and Jasper.

                    PATRICIA
          What can I say?

                    JASPER
          'My hero' would be okay.

                    PATRICIA
          Oh... my hero.

EXT. ROSARITA HOTEL - PARKING LOT - DAY

Jasper's Cadillac and Daisy's station wagon pull into the
courtyard. The kids and Patricia empty out of the station
wagon. Jasper is BLOWING the HORN.

INT. HOTEL ROOM

Daisy, on the phone, listening. Clearly upset. From
outside we hear the HORN BLOWING. She hangs up, walks to
the window, peers out.

DAISY'S POV

She sees the kids, Patricia and Jasper waving up to her.

ANGLE ON DAISY

Leaning out the window, waving.

                    DAISY
          I'll be right down.

EXT. ROSARITA HOTEL - PARKING LOT - DAY

Daisy is embracing Amanda.

                    DAISY
          I'll never let you out of my sight
          again.

                    PATRICIA
          He did it, Daze, he did it.

Daisy looks up at Jasper.

                    DAISY
          I'll always be grateful.

EXT. ROSARITA BEACH HOTEL - PATIO - DAY

Below the patio is a pool, and all sorts of people are
sitting around having cocktails. Lots of servicemen.
Amanda and Skipper are playing in the shallow end.

Jasper and Patricia are sitting at a table on the patio.
Patricia takes her glasses off.

                    JASPER
          You met Daisy back east, in
          school, didn't you?

                    PATRICIA
          We were at Goucher together. And
          Mark, my... her brother, was at
          Annapolis...
                    (MORE)

                    PATRICIA (CONT'D)
          We used to go there for weekends.
          Daisy met Bill who was a friend of
          Mark's... they proposed to us the
          same night... and he knew we would
          say yes...

                    JASPER
          Did you have one of those weddings
          with swords?

                    PATRICIA
          Oh, yes. And the honeymoon, too.
          But it was only a week. A few days
          at the Greenbriar and then
          Washington and then he joined the
          Arizona in Honolulu...

Jasper absently picks up her glasses and puts them on.

                    JASPER
          Tell me about the swords... Oh, my
          God.

                    PATRICIA
          What is it?

                    JASPER
          Look over there.

He points, she looks a few feet away to the pool.

PATRICIA'S POV (OUT OF FOCUS)

Sees the exact .sight she saw when her aunt was killed -
a man in white, a blur, leaning over someone in a chair.

                                        BACK TO SCENE

Patricia stifles a scream.

                    PATRICIA
          I saw it again!!

                    JASPER
          Right.

                    PATRICIA
          What happened at the pool, to Aunt
          Susan.

                    JASPER
          Now put on your glasses. What do
          you see?

                    PATRICIA
              (she puts her glasses
               on)
          A man in a wheelchair, and a guy
          giving him a drink.

                    JASPER
          I guess you have to be blind to
          see it.

                    PATRICIA
          Right. If I take off my glasses,
          he's Andrew and the man in the
          wheelchair is Aunt Susan.

                    JASPER
          ... That's it! 'You'd have to be
          blind to see it.' The person who
          killed your aunt waited until you
          were swimming because he wanted
          you to see him -- but not
          recognize him. Just enough to make
          it look like Andrew did it.

                    PATRICIA
          Someone who knew me.

She looks out at the pool again.

                    JASPER
              What is it?

                    PATRICIA
              Nothing.

                    JASPER
          You know who it is?

                    PATRICIA
          No. I don't have a clue.

EXT. ROSARITA HOTEL - PARKING LOT - DAY

Jasper, Patricia, Daisy, Amanda and Skipper. One of the
hotel boys is finishing polishing Jasper's car. He tips
him. Now that they are all ready to leave, who goes with
whom in what car is an issue. Skipper settles it by
climbing into Jasper's car.

                    SKIPPER
          I want to go with Jasper.

                    PATRICIA
          I think we should all go with
          Daisy...

                    SKIPPER
          No!

And he grabs the steering wheel for emphasis.

                    DAISY
          You guys go ahead. Why don't we
          meet for lunch... Pepe's... do you
          know it?

                    JASPER
          It's across from the bullring.

                    DAISY
          It'll be a nice stopping place.

INT. JASPER'S CAR - DAY

Jasper, Patricia and Skipper are driving into Tijuana.

                    SKIPPER
          I gotta go.

He means to the bathroom.

                    JASPER
          It's just over there.

INT. PEPE'S RESTAURANT - DAY

They're all sitting at a table -- Jasper and Patricia are
at opposite ends of the table. Skipper, Daisy and Amanda
sit between them. Patricia is the only one who can see
Jasper's parked Cadillac out the window.

                    JASPER
          You know I was here once -- right
          across the street-- I saw
          Manolette. He was so beautiful.
          The way he stood -- let me show
          you.
               (to Skipper) You be
                the bull.

                    AMANDA
          I want to be a bull, too.

> JASPER
> You can be a bullette.

Jasper demonstrates to the kids how to be a bull.

> JASPER (CONT'D)
> Okay. He fought one bull -- I'll
> fight two.

He stands in matador's pose.

> JASPER (CONT'D)
> Ee-ha-tora! If I wasn't going to
> be a screenwriter -- I was going
> to be a bullfighter.

The kids -- "bulls" -- charge Jasper, who deftly escapes
them. The kids love this. Jasper dodges and ducks and now
is in a position to see out the window.

> JASPER (CONT'D)
> fucr!

JASPER'S POV

He sees a Mexican man trying to pry open the trunk of the
Cadillac with a crowbar.

BACK TO SCENE

> JASPER
> Get the police!

He heads for the door.

EXT. STREET - DAY

Jasper comes barreling out of the door. The Mexican man
races across the street, dodging cars, and disappears
under the huge outside structure of the bullfight arena.
Jasper follows.

ARENA - DAY

Under the huge iron beams and wood struts of the circular
arena. The place is deserted, the ticket booths are
boarded up; the light filters through cracks like search
lights and the beams throw crisscrossed shadows on
everything. The effect is ominous and confusing. Jasper
looks around, listens. Suddenly, he hears a GATE CLANG.
He runs off in that direction.

ANGLE

An old swinging gate, a loose chain and an ancient
padlock securing it to a pipe. There's room, however, for
Jasper to squeeze through.

Now he's in a lower part of the arena.

Long, dark, circular corridors, illuminated by tiny
shafts of light through cracked ceilings above. Jasper
walks carefully -- listening for his prey -- listening.
Suddenly: A GUNSHOT. The bullet slams into a wall, just
inches from his head.

JASPER

Ducks down low. Another SHOT -- he turns a corner, he's
in another corridor. This one is lined on both sides with
cages -- in the cages are tomorrow's bulls. They are not
happy where they are. Jasper hears FOOTSTEPS.

He reaches up and hoists himself off the floor. A moment
later, below him, the Mexican man appears, gun in hand.

Jasper allows him to traverse the length of the corridor,
then lowers himself to the floor. The man turns, sees
Jasper. Very calmly, deliberately, he raises the PISTOL
at Jasper, FIRES, Jasper hits the floor. He rolls over
and in the same motion unlocks one of the bull cages. A
huge black bull bolts out into the corridor between
Jasper and the gunman.

BULL

Looks at Jasper, looks at the gunman. The gunman is
framed in the bright Mexican sunlight. To the bull, it
means freedom. He lowers his head and charges.

GUNMAN

He FIRES wildly at the rushing bull. To no avail. He
drops the GUN and rushes outside. The bull takes off
after him. Jasper lowers himself to the floor -- in time
to hear very LOUD SCREAMING. Jasper runs to the end of
the corridor, past the BELLOWING and pawing of the angry
BULLS.

EXT. BULLRING - DAY

Jasper emerges into the sunlight and the sand of the
arena.

Jasper -- shocked, horror.

JASPER'S POV

He sees the bull, with his horns, tossing the limp,
bloodied body of the gunman into the air, again and
again. There is nothing Jasper can do.

Then, all at once, the bull stops. His legs buckle· under
him, then fold, and the bull sits down, mortally wounded
by the gunshots. A moment, then it falls over, blood
pouring out of its inert body onto the sand.

JASPER

Walks out to the two corpses. He kneels down, rolls the
man face-upwards.

                         PATRICIA (O.S.)
             Jasper!

Jasper turns. Patricia and two uniformed policemen
approach. Jasper stands up, takes her around the
shoulders.

                         PATRICIA (CONT'D)
             Who is he?

EXT. DAISY'S HOUSE (LA JOLLA) - DAY

Jasper and Patricia have just arrived. Skipper is hauling
a teddy bear to the house.

                         PATRICIA
             Will you call me from Los Angeles?

                         JASPER
             Of course. Patricia, there's
             something fishy about this. How
             did that guy know the money was in
             the trunk?

                         PATRICIA
             How do you know he knew? That's
             where people put their valuables
             ... don't they?

                         JASPER
             What if he knew? Patricia... what
             if someone told him? What if he's
             the one? The one who killed
             Andrew?

                    PATRICIA
Don't be ridiculous. The police
said he's a local thug. He's never
been across the border.

                    JASPER
Come to L.A. with me... but don't
stay here, something's wrong here.

                    PATRICIA
Wrong?

                    JASPER
Patricia, I don't trust Daisy.

                    PATRICIA
What are you saying? She's my best
friend. She's like a sister
to me. We've known each other
since...

                    JASPER
She didn't want me to come down
here. She didn't want me to follow
you to the kidnapper. She's the
one who got all the notes...

                    PATRICIA
Look, how can you even say such a
thing. You saw how she was. She
was hysterical! They took her
child too! She was ready to sell
her jewels...

                    JASER
She had already sold them... I saw
them -- in a jewelry store in
Hollywood. Those are fake.

                    PATRICIA
No. Stop. This is too much. Too
much, Jasper. Not another word.

                    JASPER
You're just as myopic about Daisy
as you are without your glasses.
Can't you see, she's...

                    PATRICIA
You're so used to inventing cheap
thrillers, you can't even imagine
genuine friendship -- You're
saying Daisy would be involved in
murder, kidnapping? ...
                    (MORE)

> PATRICIA (CONT'D)
> You just have too much Hollywood
> in your brains to think straight.

> JASPER
> Maybe Daisy's husband is involved
> in this.

> PATRICIA
> Don't be ridiculous, he's in the
> Philippines.

> JASPER
> How do you know? Maybe he's home.
> Maybe it wasn't someone
> impersonating an officer maybe it
> was an officer.

> PATRICIA
> Jasper, this is insane. You're
> talking about my best friend.
> I won't hear it anymore.

> JASPER
> I'm your best friend.

> PATRICIA
> Jasper. Go away. Leave me alone.
> I don't walk to talk to you
> anymore.

She folds her arms over her chest, locks her jaw and
that's that.

> JASPER
> Patricia.

> PATRICIA
> No. Just go.

Jasper is helpless. She turns and walks away. Jasper gets
in the Cadillac and drives off.

ANGLE - PATRICIA

She watches Jasper drive away. Tears in her eyes.

EXT. SAN DIEGO NAVAL HQ - DAY

Jasper's red Cadillac stops at the gate house. A young
cadet points out directions, Jasper drives off.

EXT. NAVAL RECORDS BUILDING - ESTABLISHING SHOT - DAY

Jasper approaches on foot, enters.

INT. NAVAL RECORDS BUILDING - DAY

Jasper walks up to a WAVE, seated behind a reception
desk.

                         WAVE
          May I help you?

                         JASPER
          I hope so. My brother-in-law...
          he's missing... I mean, not
          missing in action or anything.
          Just missing. And my sister is
          very... I mean, the war ll over,
          right?

                         WAVE
          It's in all the papers.

                         JASPER
          Then why can't he come home? Or
          maybe he is home and... won't come
          home.

                         WAVE
          It happens. There's no law says he
          has to.

                         JASPER
          He's supposed to be on the
          Philadelphia... in Manila.

                         WAVE
          Third door on the right. But it
          hasn't sailed.

                         JASPER
               (starts to go, then
                turns)
          Let me ask you a question.

                         WAVE
          Four-thirty. And I have gas
          coupons. It's your eyes.

                         JASPER
          May I take a raincheck?

                    WAVE
          The other question?

                    JASPER
          If he wanted t...could he get
          home... back to the States --
          Another way? Not on his ship?

                    WAVE
          It's been done. Is he an officer?

                    JASPER
          Commander.

                    WAVE
          Doubt it. There's ten divisions of
          angry G.I.'s stalled in Manila
          Bay... I think the minimum rank to
          jump the line is Admiral. Still.

                    JASPER
          Anything's possible?

                    WAVE
          Well, not anything -- but I'm here
          every day.

She is cute enough so that if he weren't so preoccupied,
he might think twice.

Jasper moves on to a corridor, counts the doors, enters
the third. This one is filled with clerk/typists behind a
wall-to-wall counter. The person in charge is a CHIEF
PETTY OFFICER. Lots of ribbons, and bored -- probably
relieved to see a new face.

                    C.P.O.
          How ya doin'?

                    JASPER
          Just fine, thanks, yourself?

                    C.P.O.
          I can't complain -- actually I can
          -- I went out a few times with the
          blonde -- and once with the
          redhead and they got to be good
          friends. And now neither of them
          . . . But . . .

He surveys the group of WAVE typists.

                    JASPER
          You've got no complaints.

                    C.P.O.
              (nods)
          So what can I do for you?

                    JASPER
          The <u>Philadelphia</u>?

The C.P.O. shakes his head.

                    C.P.O.
          Something, ain't it? The war's
          over and those poor bastards are
          stuck in Manila. Lots of wives
          thinking -- they ain't getting
          shot at -- what are they doing
          with their free time? Like Pearl
          before the war. Booze, broads and
          booze.

                    JASPER
          You were at Pearl?

                    C.P.O.
          The <u>Arizona</u>... You're looking at
          one very lucky fellow.

                    JASPER
          That's funny. Did you know a guy
          named Mark St. Claire? Officer.
          Right out of Annapolis?

                    C.P.O.
              (shakes his head)
          Doesn't ring a bell. You looking
          for him?

                    JASPER
          <u>No</u>. He died... maybe you know
          someone who knew him.

                    C.P.O.
          Try The Dolphin. A lot of guys
          from the hospital who got it at
          Pearl hang out there. Buy a few
          beers, you never know.

EXT. THE DOLPHIN - ESTABLISHING SHOT - DAY

A bar within walking and wheelchair distance of the Naval
Hospital. Nothing fancy. Just a bar.

INT. THE DOLPHIN - DAY

Lots of Navy stuff on the walls -- pennants, flags,
cracked photos of ships, but not particularly charming. A
few sailors at the bar, some guys in civvies. There are a
few tables, men in wheelchairs play cards, chat, drink --
it's like a day room with alcohol. Jasper is leaning over
the bar talking to the BARTENDER.

                    BARTENDER
            (pointing out men)
          Charlie, Vern,
          Willie... and Red.

This, of course, attracts the above named, and they turn
in Jasper's direction.

                    BARTENDER (CONT'D)
          He wants to know about the
          Arizona.

                    JASPER
          Not exactly... just
            one officer... (to
            the Bartender)
          What are these guys drinking?

                    BARTENDER
          I'll bring over the round.

Jasper steps down from the bar and joins two men, CHARLIE
and VERN at a table. WILLIE and RED join them.

                    JASPER
          Jasper Starkey...

The men introduce themselves.

                    RED
          I saw your name last night -- in
          the pictures. The Waco kid.

                    VERN
          You the Waco kid?

                    JASPER
          No, I wrote it.

                    VERN
          You look a lot like the Waco kid.

                    JASPER
          Thank you.

                    RED
          Hollywood... shit, I'd like to go
          there.

The Bartender brings over a round of drinks.

                    JASPER
          Hey... well, here's to...

                    CHARLIE
          The Arizona...

                    RED
          And fucking good riddance.

The other's protest this "blasphemy."

                    RED (CONT'D)
          Then to the men who went down...

All toast.

                    JASPER
          And Mark St. Claire?

The men look at each other, searching their memories.
Finally.

                    WILLIE
          I knew the prick. Academy... Put
          you on report just for the fun of
          it. Everyone hated him.

                    RED
               (to Jasper) A friend
                of yours?

                    JASPER
          I never knew him. Friend of a
          friend.
               (to Willie) Tell me
                more.

                    WILLIE
          What's to tell?

                    JASPER
          How did he die?

                    WILLIE
          Who says he died?

                    JASPER
          The U.S. government. It's in a
          telegram.

                    WILLIE
          Well, they wouldn't lie, would
          they?

                    JASPER
          What're you getting at, Willie?

                    WILLIE
          Sunday morning. He was still on
          shore.

                    WILLIE (CONT'D)
          Probably drunk in some cathouse in
          Honolulu. I figure he either
          pulled it together to make
          it back to the ship in time to die
          -- or he didn't.

Jasper's stunned.

                    JASPER
          No shit.

                    WILLIE
          Yeah, no shit.

EXT. DAISY'S HOUSE (LA JOLLA)

The Plymouth slides up silently to the street overlooking
the ranch.

INT. PATRICIA'S BEDROOM - NIGHT

Patricia is sleeping. Skipper comes into her room.

                    SKIPPER
          Mommy. Mommy, wake up.

Patricia stirs, wakens.

                    SKIPPER (CONT'D)
          Daddy's here.

                    PATRICIA
          Darling, is someone...

                    SKIPPER
          He's here. I saw him -- outside
          -- from my window.

                    PATRICIA
          Skipper...

                    SKIPPER
          Will he give me a ride on a
          donkey? Come and see, come on,
          Mommy.

He tugs on her hand.

Patricia rises, puts on a robe, takes a flashlight off
the dressing table, and follows Skipper out the bedroom
door...

HALLWAY

and DOWN the stairs TO the living room. It's dark and
ominous, but Patricia doesn't turn on any lights.

                    SKIPPER (CONT'D)
          He's outside, Mommy.

They make their way outside. A full moon and a couple of
lights over the barn provide illumination. In the
driveway, parked behind Daisy's station wagon, is the old
Plymouth we have seen so often.

                    SKIPPER (CONT'D)
          Over there, Mommy.

Patricia puts her finger on her lips.

                    PATRICIA
          We have to be very quiet, darling.

                    SKIPPER
          Because it's a surprise?

                    PATRICIA
          Yes. It's a surprise.

This delights Skipper, so he puts his finger over his
lips, too. They step off the porch, and continue on. Past
the bar, the empty swimming pool, and down a path.

ANGLE

Ahead of them, across an avocado grove, is a large tool/ equipment set. There is light coming from the one window.

                    SKIPPER
          I saw him go there, Mommy.

Patricia turns on the flashlight as they make their way between the rows of avocado trees. The Santa Anas suddenly whip down from the deserts and blow through the trees, twisting their shapes against the moonlight.

ANGLE - SHACK

Weathered, tattered, it looms ahead, ugly and forbidding. Skipper and Patricia are almost there -- just twenty feet away.

                    PATRICIA
          I want you to wait here.

                    SKIPPER
          Why, Mommy?

                    PATRICIA
          For the surprise. Will you be
          scared?

                    SKIPPER
          No.

                    PATRICIA
          Good. You wait here, okay?

                    SKIPPER
              (trying hard not to
               laugh)
          Okay.

Patricia hands him the flashlight and forges ahead until she is at the shack. She creeps to the window and slowly lifts herself up for a look.

PATRICIA'S POV

She sees the interior of the shack -- rusted and dusty tools on a workbench, cans of paint, a few rakes and hoes lean against yellowing walls. The room is empty of people.

ANGLE ON PATRICIA

Searching the room. Suddenly --

                    MALE VOICE (O.S.)
          Hello, Patricia.

She whips around.

Standing there is a MAN dressed in a Navy officer's
uniform.

                    PATRICIA
          Mark?

A gleeful Skipper rushes up to Patricia.

                    SKIPPER
          Surprise, Mommy! Surprise. See,
          Daddy's here.

                    MARK
          I'm home, darling. Home from the
          war. Aren't you happy to see me?

Daisy moves INTO VIEW.

                    PATRICIA
          I don't understand.

                    MARK
          I'm alive and well... Shouldn't we
          celebrate?

No answer.

                    MARK (CONT'D)
          Oh. Well, you see... I didn't die.
          The Arizona went down and
          fortunately I wasn't on it. I
          grabbed a freighter to Ensenada
          and spent the next three years in
          Mexico. Forgive me for not writing
          -- the mail is hopeless, anyway.
          Isn't it, sis?

Daisy steps forward.

                    DAISY
          Yes.

                    PATRICIA
          What is he talking about, Daisy?
          Daisy, tell me.

                    DAISY
          He's a deserter -- he deserted
          from the war. It's a capital
          offense. They could hang him.

                    MARK
          No G.I. bill for me. I need money,
          wife. I need money to travel, to
          live well... to bribe people.

                    PATRICIA
          You killed Aunt Susan.

Mark is non-committal.

                    PATRICIA (CONT'D)
          You knew I couldn't recognize your
          face... but you could make me
          think it was Andrew.
               (She looks to Daisy)
          Daisy, say something. Something,
          damn it.

Daisy looks at her hard, right at her.

                    DAISY
          She was a mean, ungenerous woman.
          She hated it when our life was
          going good and loved it when it
          wasn't. She stuck her nose in the
          air and kept her hand out of her
          purse. You know what she said to
          me when I asked her for money
          against my jewelry? She gave me
          the address of a jeweler in
          Hollywood. Good riddance.

First Mark, then Skipper begin to laugh.

                    PATRICIA
          Skipper, come here.

Skipper is torn.

                    MARK
          Go on. Go to your mommy.

Skipper hesitates. Mark pushes him.

                    MARK (CONT'D)
          Go on.

All of a sudden Skipper is afraid of Mark. He rushes to
Patricia and clutches her thigh.

                    PATRICIA
          It was you... you took the
          children.

Mark smiles weakly.

She leaps on him, her fists flailing.

                    PATRICIA (CONT'D)
          You wanted my money? You kidnapped
          my child! You are a bastard! You
          are a murderer!

Skipper is screaming, Daisy is trying to pull Patricia
away. Mark punches her solidly in the stomach and she
falls off him and sinks to her knees, gasping for air.

                    MARK
          Homecomings are always so
          emotional. Now, let's all calm
          down. I can't live in the good old
          U.S.A., wife. I will go away. To a
          foreign land and then I will only
          be a distant, financial...
          inconvenience.

                    PATRICIA
          No.

                    MARK
          But, wife... You know what I am
          capable of. There is always plan
          B. You will be eliminated and I
          think Daisy gets Skipper... and
          eventually when something terrible
          happens to the lad... all the
          money.

Patricia is too stunned to speak.

                    MARK (CONT'D)
          Patricia, darling. Time runs out.

                    PATRICIA
          All right.

                    MARK
          Let's start with the fifty
          thousand.

                    JASPER (O.S.)
          She doesn't have it.

ANGLE ON JASPER

                    JASPER
          I do. And you're not getting it.

                                        BACK TO SCENE

Jasper stands there, holding his Colt .45.

                    JASPER (CONT'D)
          And I brought this to make sure.

                    PATRICIA
          Jasper. It was him. All the time.
          He did everything... He killed.

                    JASPER
          I know, honey. But it's all over
          now.

                    MARK
          Oh, Christ.

He pulls out a gun. Points it at Jasper.

                    MARK (CONT'D)
          We do have a problem. Who shoots
          first.

                    JASPER
          I do.

Jasper SHOOTS Mark in the chest. It sends him flying back
and to the ground. Jasper retrieves Mark's pistol.

                    MARK
          You are always there. Always...
          Christ, I'm dying.
          (to Patricia)
          Have you told him yet? Our secret?

                    PATRICIA
          No.

                    MARK
          Tell him. Tell him about your
          bastard child.
                    (to Jasper)
          It's not mine. You know, I would
          have shot you, if you'd given me
          half a chance.

Daisy rushes forward to him, cradling his head.

                    DAISY
          Mark...

                    MARK
          Daisy, darling. Facing the sea
          would be nice... under an old
          avocado tree? And I'll be... still
          the hero, right?

                    DAISY
          Oh, Mark.

                    MARK
          And it'll just be as if I... never
          came back.

He dies.

Jasper moves to Patricia, holds her and Skipper. Daisy
lowers Mark to the ground. Daisy looks up.

                    DAISY
          Will you help me? Please help me.

                    JASPER
                    (to Patricia)
          Take Skipper to the house.

He steps forward, bends down and picks up Mark.

                    JASPER (CONT'D)
          (to Daisy) Show me.

Daisy steps ahead as they make their way through the
avocado groves.

HIGH SHOT

As the dawn breaks, the rising sun illuminates Daisy,
followed by Jasper bearing the lifeless body of Mark
towards the bluff overlooking the ocean. And Patricia
leading Skipper back to the house.

                                        DISSOLVE TO:

EXT. PACIFIC COAST HIGHWAY - JASPER'S CADILLAC - DAY

Jasper driving, Patricia in the passenger seat. She turns
and looks at Skipper, asleep in the back seat.

                    PATRICIA
          What he said...

                    JASPER
          It doesn't matter.

                    PATRICIA
          Yes, it does. It's how he could
          justify what he did... Our wedding
          night in Washington. He couldn't
          make love to me. So he beat me.
          I ran away... and... I met... I
          was rescued by this soldier. I
          stayed with him that night. He
          went off... he never even knew my
          name.

                    JASPER
          It's all right.

                    PATRICIA
          It is now, isn't it?

                    JASPER
          I love you. And it is.

                    PATRICIA
          I love you, too, Jasper. I do. But
          will you tell me now?

                    JASPER
          Tell you what?

                    PATRICIA
          About your limp. How were you
          wounded?

                    JASPER
          Surfing.

                    PATRICIA
          I don't know what surfing is.

                    JASPER
          I'll show you.

                                        FADE OUT.

               THE END

"T H E   F L U T E"

Screenplay by

Michael Elias

and

Eve Babitz

FADE IN:

WATER

As the CAMERA PULLS BACK we see it is an indoor swimming
pool. Daylight filters through the skylight as a solitary
SWIMMER does laps with an ever-increasing intensity.

LIFEGUARD

Immersed in a book, oblivious to the swimmer.

SWIMMER

He weakens. Total exhaustion overtakes him. He flails,
begins to drown.

LIFEGUARD

Still reading.

SWIMMER

He manages a SHOUT, and goes down for the last time as a
thousand bubbles burst on the water.

LIFEGUARD

He hears the sound of the bubbles, looks up, tosses the book
aside, and dives into the pool.

EXT. PARIS STREET - DAY

An ambulance, klaxon bellowing, makes its way through
traffic. It comes to an intersection. A traffic jam forces
it to stop.

AMBULANCE

The doors open and the swimmer steps out, still in his
bathing suit, clutching his clothes. He waves a 'thank you'
to the attendants and runs out into the traffic.

EXT. HOTEL - DAY

The swimmer, BILLY SAWYER, still holding his clothes, jogs
into this small, unassuming Left Bank hotel.

INT. HOTEL - DAY

Billy's in his middle thirties, seemingly trustworthy, and,
from his perfect accent, American.

As Billy taps impatiently on the desk, the concierge,
CLAUDE, shuffles to his mailbox. Claude hands Billy his key
and a message.

                         BILLY
             I can't read this.
                   (handing it back
                    to Claude)

                        CLAUDE
          Mister Pitkin. He called twice.

                         BILLY
          Never heard of him.

Billy dashes up the stairs, a man in a hurry.

INT. HOTEL ROOM - DAY

While Billy is in the shower, the CAMERA explores the room
of this American in Paris. Too much stuff for a tourist;
stuff that a businessman wouldn't carry around: a VHS
attached to the TV, a micro-component stereo unit, stacks of
cassettes, books, camera equipment, lots of clothes, a few
framed posters and prints leaning against the walls. It's
the hotel room of a man who has recently left his wife.

Billy steps out of the bathroom, drying himself. He dresses
quickly in conservative Parachute. He moves to the mirror
for a final look. Not content, he adjusts a hair, scrapes a
tooth, stretches out a wrinkle, and despairs. He repeats
the process, trying to make himself perfect, and comes
closer this time. Somewhat satisfied, he bolts out of the
room. A moment later he reappears. He forgot his wallet.

EXT. HOTEL - DAY

Billy bounds out of the hotel, starts left, changes his
mind, goes right.

EXT. PARIS STREETS - LEFT BANK - DAY

Billy, always in a hurry, making his way through the mid-day
crowds this lovely spring day. Every once in a while he
stops in front of a store window to make sure he is still the
same person who started out on this mission. He is.

EXT. CAFE DEUX MAGOTS - DAY

Billy arrives in a big hurry, scans the customers seated
outside and sees a gorgeous blonde WOMAN paying her check
inside.

INT. CAFE DEUX MAGOTS - DAY

Billy nearly catches up with the woman, but she leaves by
another door.

EXT. CAFE DEUX MAGOTS - DAY

Billy catches up with this woman outside and, in front of
everyone, touches her shoulder and calls out:

                         BILLY
          Lise!

The woman turns around and surprises him by not being Lise,
and gives him a whithering look.

Billy, stunned, stands there as everyone watches, amused.

Just then another tall, gorgeous blonde appears, and it's
LISE, a twenty-nine-year-old French model wearing very hip
Santa Fe American clothes. Her greeting is perfunctory,
almost formal.

INT. CAFE DEUX MAGOTS

They sit down together at a table. Billy smiles at her. It
doesn't help. She looks tense. There is a pause.

                         LISE
          I am sorry... the traffic.

                         BILLY
          Oh! It's okay. Me, too. So, how
          are you?

                    LISE
Busy.

                    BILLY
Good. That's good. But, I mean,
are you okay? I worry about you
being in the apartment all by
yourself. If you're safe, you
know... I worry about you--

                    LISE
          (sighs)
Yes, I'm okay. And I was okay
this morning when you called and I
was also okay before lunch when
you called again. I'm okay, okay?
God, I hate that word 'okay'.

                    BILLY
I don't know... you look tense.

                    LISE
Will you get to the point, please?

                    BILLY
The point?

                    LISE
You told me you had something very
important to tell me. What is it?

Billy smiles. He searches his pockets, taking his time.
Finally takes out a piece of paper that he unfolds and
places on the table in front of Lise. There is a name and
phone number written on it.

                    LISE
          (looking at the paper)
What is it?

                    BILLY
I found him.

                    LISE
Who?

                    BILLY
A plumber. For the bathtub.

                    LISE
          You made me come all the way here
          just to give me the name of a
          plumber?

                    BILLY
          He's not just a plumber. He's
          supposed to be great. And I
          thought it would be better to
          discuss it with you in person, you
          know... have a little talk...
          about plumbing... and us...

                    LISE
          Billy, we are trying to--

At this moment, the WAITER appears.

                    WAITER
          Vous désirez, monsieur... madame?

                    BILLY
          What will you have, darling?

                    LISE
               (looking at her watch)
          Nothing.

                    BILLY
          Nothing? Oh, I know... let's have
          champagne, what the hell! You
          still love champagne, don't you?

Lise does not reply.

                    BILLY
               (continuing; to the waiter)
          Champagne!

                    LISE
          Tea.

                    WAITER
          Champagne and tea.

                    LISE
          Billy... we are trying to be
          separated, for Christ's sake.

                    BILLY
I know. And it's not working out.
          (a beat)
Why don't we just get back
together?

                    LISE
Because we were never _really_ happy
together, and you know it.

                    BILLY
Really happy? I was happy. You
were happy.

                    LISE
Maybe you were happy, but I
wasn't.

                    BILLY
You were happy. I remember you
used to say all the time: "Oh,
Billy, I'm so happy!" Remember
going to the movies in Times
Square? Remember the trip to Key
West? Remember... uh... remember
Baltimore? Those soft-shell crab
sandwiches? You were happy.

                    LISE
I thought I was happy but I
wasn't.

                    BILLY
What do you mean, you _thought_ you
were happy?

                    LISE
Just what I said.

                    BILLY
Well, let me tell you something.
You don't look very happy now.

                    LISE
It's not a matter of being happy
or not.

                    BILLY
          (puzzled)
It isn't?

                    LISE
          Billy, I don't want to have any
          more of these conversations. And
          I don't think we should talk for a
          while, unless... it's really
          important.

                    BILLY
               (sad)
          Well... plumbing is important.
          But, if that's the way you want
          it--

                    LISE
               (getting up)
          I need some time. Just let me
          have some time to think, okay?

                    BILLY
          Sure. To think about what?

Lise, angered, walks out, almost bumping into the waiter, who
is bringing the champagne. The paper is still lying on the
table. Billy jumps up.

                    BILLY
          Lise! Wait! You forgot the
          plumber!

Billy quickly gets his wallet out to pay the waiter. He
doesn't find any small bills. He leaves the waiter a big
bill and rushes out without waiting for his change.

EXT. STREET - DAY

Lise proceeds down the street, Billy following her a few yards
back. She crosses the street and descends the stairs to the
Metro. Billy has difficulty crossing the street, finally
makes it across.

INT. METRO

Billy arrives at the ticket stand, looks around. She's gone.
But where? It's one of those larger stations, a maze of
tunnels, escalators, and wall posters, one of which is a
beautiful blonde extolling the virtues of milk. We recognize
her. It is Lise. Her inviting, wholesome smile beckons to
Billy. He heads off in her direction, hoping that the
artificial will lead to the authentic.

ESCALATOR

Billy descending.

PLATFORM

Billy arrives as a train pulls out. This is hopeless. Billy
turns and walks towards the exit and the SOUNDS, growing
louder, of a CHAMBER ENSEMBLE.

Billy hears it. In the Metro?

TUNNELS

Billy walking, lost. The exits don't seem to exit. The MUSIC
continues, leading him closer to its source.

BILLY'S POV

A blonde passes by ahead of him. Lise?

BILLY

He speeds up, heading for her. He arrives at a larger
platform. The MUSIC is louder. The blonde is gone. WE SEE
the MUSICIANS.

MUSICIANS

A small chamber ensemble. A sign on an easel explains that
they are playing for the pleasure of the Metro users,
courtesy of the City of Paris.

BILLY

Looking at the musicians. For the moment, captivated.

ISOBEL

She plays the flute. It is the first time we see her.
Anyone with an appreciation of true beauty will never forget
her. Billy does not see her. He is denied that pleasure
for the moment.

BILLY

Takes in the music for a moment, then turns and heads for an
exit sign. Along the way, he passes a man who is reading a
magazine. On the back cover, staring at Billy, is Lise. Billy
reaches down, takes the magazine from the man, tears off the
back cover, and hands the magazine back to the startled man.
Billy wads up the page and, on his way out, tosses it as far
as he can, American style.

INT. SCREENING ROOM

SCREEN

WE SEE a commercial for perfume set against a love story of
two skiers making their way down the slopes of the
Matterhorn to Zermatt. The commercial ends with the lovers
embracing with multiple images of Swiss wildflowers breaking
through the spring snow.

The LIGHTS go on, revealing a group of people sitting around
a conference table. The group includes FRANK, a Frenchman
in his late forties. He owns the place.

                    FRANK
          Gentlemen, you know Billy Sawyer.
          The auteur of this spot.

Heads (three of them, all in suits, all from New York) turn.
Billy waves and acknowledges their sincere applause. PAUL is
the senior executive, MEL and JACK are the rest of the team.

                    MEL
          You shoot it, Billy?

                    FRANK
          He did everything but act in it.

                    PAUL
          Gorgeous.

                    BILLY
          Thanks. What've you guys got?

                    PAUL
          Lipstick and Stacey Doyle.

                    BILLY
          I've heard of lipstick.

Paul presses a remote button.

                        PAUL
                  (to Frank)
            Could you get the lights, Frank?

The room darkens and a commercial comes on the screen.

                        MEL
            Latè says she turned their whole
            teen line around. She's hot.

As the commercial unspools, it is clear why. Stacey is
quite stunning. Her lips scream out "buy what is on them".
However, the commercial-- It ends. LIGHTS go on.

                        PAUL
            This time, we want Paris, Billy.

                        BILLY
            You'll get Paris.

                        FRANK
            You'll get Paris like you've never
            gotten it before.

                        BILLY
            Two things: I want to move her
            around a lot.

                        MEL
            Great. And...?

                        BILLY
            I don't want her.

There's a silence. No one knows what to say. Billy
continues.

                        BILLY
                  (continuing)
            She's got a bad left side. Her
            eyes are too small.

                        FRANK
            I like her.

                        JACK
            Maybe he's kidding.

                    MEL
          No, he's not.

                    BILLY
          You guys see the milk ads around
          the city?

They all shake their heads 'no'.

                    BILLY
               (continuing)
          Check 'em out. I think she's the
          girl we want.

                    PAUL
          Billy--

                    BILLY
          Just check her out. I'll do some
          tests.

                    PAUL
          Billy, I don't want to argue this.

                    BILLY
          Why not? I'm the director. I
          don't have a right to say who's in
          my spot? She's a lox. She's a
          turn-off. I don't think she
          shoots well.

                    PAUL
          Billy, we're paying her a million
          dollars a year.

                    BILLY
          You didn't let me finish. For
          this product, she's perfect.

There is a moment of silence, then the U.S. guys all start
laughing. Billy joins in. Frank, too.

INT. FRANK'S OFFICE - DAY

Frank is pacing. Billy is sifting through some storyboards.

                    FRANK
          You were trying to put your
          wife in their commercial.

                    BILLY
          I happen to think she would be
          very good.

                    FRANK
          You think she would be very
          grateful and come back to you.
          They thought you were absolutely
          crazy.

                    BILLY
          I am. I'm a crazy genius.

                    FRANK
          They don't let crazy people direct
          million dollar commercials
          anymore. Listen, you have to get
          on with your life. You have to
          forget about Lise. Get yourself a
          girlfriend. I don't know... a
          hobby, get a new place. But don't
          do anything else to put me out of
          business.

                    BILLY
               (considers this, then:)
          You know what?

                    FRANK
          What?

                    BILLY
          I think you're right.

INT. OLD CHARMING APARTMENT - DAY

It's a one-bedroom apartment with a fireplace and a view of
a small park. Billy looks around. SOPHIE, a real estate
agent and a friend, waits for his opinion.

                    BILLY
          Nice.

                    SOPHIE
          It's very quiet, too.

                    BILLY
               (looking out the window)
          I love the park.

                    SOPHIE
          It's really perfect for a
          bachelor.

Billy's expression changes abruptly. It hits him that he is
going to be living alone now. He looks panicked.

                    BILLY
          A bachelor, huh?

Billy looks around nervously.

                    BILLY
          It's a little dark.

                    SOPHIE
          Are you kidding? It's facing
          south.

                    BILLY
               (hesitating)
          I'll tell you what... it's a bit
          too small, you know?
                    (spreads his arms
                     to illustrate what
                     he's saying)

INT. VAST MODERN APARTMENT - DAY

Billy and Sophie and the LANDLADY, a woman in her fifties,
very business-like and straight-looking, enter a large,
modern, and very light apartment with a mezzanine and a view
on the Seine. A dream apartment. A large smile appears on
Billy's face as he looks around. The landlady speaks
French. [Subtitles if necessary.]

                    LANDLADY
          La salle de séjour.

                    SOPHIE
               (to Billy)
          It's huge.

Billy doesn't say a word. He keeps looking around, enjoying
the place. They enter a large, fully-equipped kitchen.

                    LANDLADY
          La cuisine est entièrement equipée.
          La cuisinière programmable... four
          à micro-onde... machine à laver la
          vaisselle... vide ordure,
          naturellement--

                    BILLY
          That's perfect.

                    LANDLADY
          Monsieur est americain?

                    BILLY
          Oui, oui... americain.

                    LANDLADY
          Par ici, s'il vous plaît.

She leads them to the master bedroom, which also has a
breathtaking view of the Seine.

                    BILLY
          Oh, my God, look at that!

                    LANDLADY
               (to Billy)
          Et vous êtes dans quelle branche?

Billy pays no attention. He's fascinated by the view.

                    SOPHIE
          It est un metteur en scène... du
          cinéma.

                    LANDLADY
               (she doesn't like
                the answer)
          Ah! Le cinéma!. Je ne sais
          pas... Nous avons beaucoup d'ennui
          avec les gens de cinéma. Ils ne
          sont pas très sérieux.

                    SOPHIE
          Mais Monsieur Sawyer est très
          sérieux...

                    LANDLADY
          Oui... C'est ce qu'ils disent tous.

Billy doesn't pay attention to the conversation. He walks out
of the room, still daydreaming. The sound of the
conversation between Sophie and the landlady fades out.

Billy is facing the door of the kitchen. All of a sudden, he
sees Lise coming out, looking gorgeous in a white nightgown,
holding a cup of coffee in her elegant hand.

                    LISE
          Billy, it's perfect. I love it.
          I think I could be really happy here.

Billy looks back at Sophie and the landlady, then back to
the kitchen door. Of course, Lise is not there anymore. He
had just imagined it. He addresses the women.

                    BILLY
          It's perfect. We... I love it.
          I'll take it!

Billy takes out his checkbook and a pen. He's ready to sign
the check.

                    BILLY
               (to landlady)
          How much? Combien?

                    SOPHIE
          You're nuts.

                    LANDLADY
               (to Sophie)
          Voyons... huit mille francs par
          mois. Premier mois, dernier
          mois... un mois de garantie...
          quatre mille francs dépot...

                    SOPHIE
          Hope you know what you're doing.
          Three months at eight thousand
          francs a month, plus four thousand
          francs cleaning deposit. That's
          twenty-eight thousand francs.

Billy writes the check without batting an eyelash and hands
it to the landlady.

                    LANDLADY
               (scrutinizing the check)
          C'est exact.

                    SOPHIE
          I've got to run.

Billy shakes hands with the landlady and leads her and Sophie
to the door.

                    BILLY
          Merci.

                    LANDLADY
          Merci a vous. C'est un grand
          plaisir de faire des affaires avec
          vous.

Sophie is going to translate but Billy motions her not to
bother. He closes the door and, leaning on it, takes a big
breath. Then he rushes to the phone. He dials and waits
anxiously for a second. Lise's voice is heard.

                    BILLY
          Lise? Now listen to me. Yes, it
          is very, very important. I just
          rented a fantastic new
          apartment... for us. Hello?

WE HEAR a click and then a dial tone. She has obviously hung up.

Billy slowly puts the receiver down and looks around. He
seems to feel lonely in this big apartment.

EXT. BILLY'S BUILDING - DAY

Billy emerges, looks around, tries to get his bearings in his
new and sudden neighborhood.

EXT. STREET - DAY

Billy, carrying groceries, is walking. He looks depressed.
He passes a music store. Instruments of all sorts are on
display in the window. The door is open, and from inside he
hears the same music he heard inside the subway (Boys
Chorus, Turandot). He stops, listens, then continues on.

EXT. STREET

Billy comes out of a bakery carrying a baguette. He wanders
aimlessly down the street.

BOOKSTORE WINDOW

Billy scans the books on display. One title attracts his
attention: "La Thérapie par la Musique" (Music As Therapy).

Billy turns away.

EXT. MUSIC STORE - DAY

Billy steps out of the music store carrying a trombone case.
The sidewalk is rather crowded. He bumps into somebody with
the case, breaks the baguette. He walks a bit, but he is
very uncomfortable. He stops, turns, and makes his way back
into the music store.

INT. MUSIC STORE - DAY

                    SALESMAN
          Yes?

                    BILLY
          You have anything smaller?

                    SALESMAN
          How small?

                    BILLY
          Very small.

The salesman hands over a piccolo.

                    SALESMAN
          There is nothing smaller.

                    BILLY
          Too small.

                    SALESMAN
          Perhaps the flute?

                    BILLY
              (thinks about it)
          The flute? perhaps.

The salesman shows him one. Assembles it. Shows him how to
hold it, and leads him to a mirror.

                    SALESMAN
          It looks very good on you.

                    BILLY
          I like flute music.

                    SALESMAN
          For me, it is the most beautiful
          of all the instruments. It is the
          most human.

                    BILLY
          Why?

                    SALESMAN
          It always has, no matter how happy
          the music, an element of sadness.

                    BILLY
          I'll take it.

                    SALESMAN
          You owe me two hundred more francs.
          I will give you a new teacher.

Billy writes another check and hands it to Lang, along with
his card.

                    BILLY
          Why don't you just have him call
          me?

Billy puts the flute case under his arm, tries walking with it.

                    BILLY
                 (continuing)
          This is definitely better.

                                        CUT TO:

INT. BILLY'S APARTMENT - DAY

Billy has finished 'furnishing'. There is a bed, a table
with two chairs, a bookcase, and everything else is on the
floor: his clothes, neatly stacked and sorted, his TV,
stereo, phone, and one plant. The art consists of a few
film posters and a framed picture of Lise, large and
beautiful enough to drive him crazy. At the moment, he is
deciding what to do with it. He does the sane thing and
slides it under the bed.

He plops down on the bed, reaches across for the phone,
begins to dial a number, then stops. He doesn't have anyone
in mind to call. He leans back and bumps his head against
the flute case. Billy opens it, assembles it. He puts it
to his mouth and tries to make a sound. No luck. He tries
a few more times without success.

He gets up and looks for a place to put the flute. He
settles on the bookcase. It does look good there. Billy
shakes his head at the stupidity of the purchase. He can't
even play it. But it does look good, so he adjusts it just
a bit, letting it catch the light.

Suddenly, he gets an idea. He dashes to the closet, drags
out a carton, and rummages through it briefly until he finds
what he's looking for: a telephone answering machine beeper.

Back to the phone. He dials with purpose. WE HEAR:

                    LISE
               [in French]
          Hello... You have reached four-
          eight-three-two-two-two-one-nine.
          I'm not in but if you leave a
          message I'll call you back.

Billy BEEPS the machine. WE HEAR a garble as the tape
rewinds, then:

                    WOMAN'S VOICE #1
               [in French]
          Lise, are you coming for dinner
          Sunday? And... I fixed the dress.
          Please let me know. Goodbye.

                    WOMAN'S VOICE #2
               [in French]
          Hello, it's Jacqueline. Do you
          want to go with me to London next
          weekend? I can get another tcket
          from Louis. We can get all our
          shopping done in one trip. Call
          me.

Then BEEP, indicating that there are no more messages.
Billy beeps the machine, rewinding the messages. He falls
back on the bed, content in the knowledge that his ex-wife
is still only talking to women. So it seems.

INT. SCREENING ROOM

Paul, Jack, and Mel are facing the screen. Frank, Billy,
and CLAUDIA, a casting director, sit behind them.

                    CLAUDIA
          We tested four actors for the
          gendarme. I think one of them,
          the last one, would also work well
          for the taxi driver. There are
          also two others for the grocer.

                    JACK
          How are their accents?

                    CLAUDIA
          Comment? I'm sorry...?

                    JACK
          They have good French accents? We
          need good French accents.

                    BILLY
          Jack, they're French.

                    JACK
          Right.

                    PAUL
              (can't believe it,
               either)
          He's just checking. Frank, could
          we roll?

Frank phones up to the projectionist.

                    FRANK
          Okay, Max.

The LIGHTS go down. ON SCREEN WE SEE a succession of actors
with weird faces, auditioning for the upcoming lipstick
commercial.

BILLY

Instantly bored. Or, more charitably, preoccupied. He digs
around in his pocket for something which interests him and
comes up with the answering machine beeper. He reaches for
the phone and quickly dials a number.

FRANK

Looks over disapprovingly.

BILLY

Motions that it's okay, his eyes are glued to the screen. A
moment later, he places the beeper over the mouthpiece and
listens. All of a sudden, his expression changes: panic,
shock. He can't believe what he's hearing. He presses the
beeper again to repeat the message. We come closer and we
can hear it, too.

                    MALE VOICE
               [in French]
          Lise... we're still on for dinner?
          I made reservations at
          L'Archestrate. Eight o'clock. I
          hope that's all right. If not,
          give me a call. Until then...

Billy beeps the phone again to rewind the message, then
slowly lowers the phone as the test reel ends and the lights
come up.

PAUL, MEL, and JACK

All turn and face Billy.

                    PAUL
          What do you think?

                    BILLY
          I think we have to be absolutely
          sure. Let's run them again.

Paul, Mel, and Jack nod their heads in agreement.

Billy looks over at Frank who, if nothing else, is
impressed.

FRANK

Picks up the phone.

                    FRANK
          Max, again.

                              CUT TO:

INT. L'ARCHESTRATE - NIGHT

The best restaurant in Paris. Billy is sitting at the bar
wearing a rather conservative but elegant suit and tie. He
keeps glancing at the door while nervously sipping a double
whisky.

Sophie walks in. He waves at her. She joins him at the
bar. They kiss each other on both cheeks, a la francaise.
He hands her a glass of champagne.

                    SOPHIE
          Congratulations!

                    BILLY
          For what?

                    SOPHIE
          Your film. It's at the
          Cinematheque Friday. You didn't
          know?

                    BILLY
          No, I knew. I have to speak
          afterwards. Answer questions. I
          don't even want to go. I made the
          damn things eighteen years ago.
               (a pause)
          Sophie, I think I made a very big
          mistake.

                    SOPHIE
          I told you the place was much too
          big for you. Oh, Billy--

                    BILLY
          Too big? Oh, no, no... not the
          apartment. It's about Lise.

                    SOPHIE
          What about Lise?

                    BILLY
          I got it all wrong. She's still
          madly in love with me but she
          doesn't know it.

                    SOPHIE
          Billy, we shouldn't talk about Lise.

                    BILLY
You're right. Just this one
thing, okay? It all came to me in
a flash. She has the weird idea
that we were unhappy together, but
she is just making it up and she
doesn't realize it. But, what's
happening now, see, is that she
really is unhappy but she doesn't
realize it, either, yet. But when
she realizes how unhappy she is
now, she will realize how happy
she was before!

                    SOPHIE
Could you repeat that?

                    BILLY
I need a favor. I have to make
her see how much she loves me, and
I have to act fast before she does
something drastic. All I have to
do is change one thing. She told
me once: "Billy, you're great,
you're bright, you're talented,
but you do one thing that turns me
off. Just one thing. If only you
could change that one thing, you
would be perfect!"

                    SOPHIE
What was it?

                    BILLY
I can't remember. I just can't
remember. You think you could ask
her? Like, what is that thing?

                    SOPHIE
Billy... there's no thing. You're
fine.
          (a beat)
You have to stop thinking about
her. Leave her alone.

At this very moment, Lise enters the restaurant with a MAN
about ten years older than she is. Billy notices them
immediately. Sophie follows Billy's look and sees Lise.

                    SOPHIE
          Oh, my God! There she is. Don't
          turn around. Let's go.

Sophie stands up. Billy is turning his back to Lise, who
sits at a distant table with her escort.

                    BILLY
          How does she look? Does she look
          happy?

Sophie turns and walks away.

EXT. L'ARCHESTRATE RESTAURANT - NIGHT

Sophie is still pulling Billy away. He keeps looking back
at Lise. She doesn't seem to have noticed him.

EXT. SAME STREET - NIGHT

SOPHIE walks fast, three steps ahead of Billy, who finally
catches up to her.

                    SOPHIE
          Did you invite me to dinner there
          because you knew she would be
          there?

                    BILLY
          Would I do something like that?
          Would I take you to a restaurant
          so I could spy on my wife? That
          would be crazy.

They walk for a while.

                    BILLY
                 (continuing)
          I wonder who the guy was.

                    SOPHIE
          Will you stop? Will you please
          get on with your life and allow
          her to have one?

                    BILLY
          Absolutely. No problem.

He stops.

                         BILLY
               Sophie... I think... all this
               excitement... I don't think I
               could eat anything.
                         (rubs his stomach)
               Don't really feel well.

                         SOPHIE
               You don't look well. Why don't we
               do this another time. Just go
               home, get some rest.

                         BILLY
               That's just what I'm going to do.
               Get some rest.

They kiss goodbye.

                                             CUT TO:

EXT. L'ARCHESTRATE RESTAURANT - NIGHT

Later, through the window pane of the restaurant, we can see
Lise and her escort getting up and heading towards the door.

WE SEE that this was Billy's POV. He's observing them,
hidden in the dark across the street from the restaurant.
He's very tense.

BILLY'S POV

Lise and the man walk out.

BILLY

Looking more and more tense.

BILLY'S POV

Lise and the man walk away.

Billy jumps out of his hiding place and follows them
discreetly, grazing the walls.

Lise and the man stop in front of a car. They have a few
words and then they shake hands. The man walks away and
Lise gets in the car.

Billy has a big smile. He feels a tremendous relief. He takes a few quick steps in the direction of Lise's car, and then stops abruptly. He is getting wiser. He backs up in the dark and watches Lise's car take off.

EXT. PARIS FLOWER MARKET - DAWN (ESTABLISHING)

Billy pulls up, parks, gets out of his car, an older Porsche convertible model, and enters.

INT. FLOWER MARKET

Billy moves from stall to stall, buying flowers until he can't carry any more.

EXT. FLOWER MARKET

Billy carries one last huge bouquet out to the car and manages to stuff it into the front seat. He squeezes into the driver's seat and starts the engine.

EXT. PARIS STREET - DAY

Billy pulls up in front of an apartment house, starts to unload the flowers and carry them into the building.

INT. BUILDING

Billy climbing the stairs, laden with flowers. He deposits them in front of an apartment door and arranges the flowers into an artistic display. He turns and heads down the stairs to get the rest of the flowers. As he disappears down the stairs, a MAN descends from the floor above and notices the flowers. He walks over, admires them, reaches down and selects one for the buttonhole in his lapel.

EXT. STREET OUTSIDE BUILDING - DAY

Billy has another armload of flowers. He pushes the car door shut with his foot.

The Man with the flower in his lapel exits the building.

Billy walks to the entrance. ANOTHER MAN passes him; he, too, has a flower in his lapel.

INT. BUILDING

Billy passes MAN #3 with a flower in his lapel, then MAN #4,
then a SCHOOLBOY carrying a small bouquet. Billy recognizes
the urgency of the situation and rushes up the stairs.

APARTMENT DOOR

An OLD WOMAN comes out of her apartment. She sees the
flowers, considers taking one, then sees Billy with his
armload.

                    OLD WOMAN
          Bonjour.

                    BILLY
          Bonjour.

                    OLD WOMAN
               Très extravagant.

Billy nods, hands her a rose, which pleases her, then
proceeds to rearrange what's left of the flowers, adding the
rest of the ones he brought up with him. When he is
satisfied, he stands back and knocks on the door. He knocks
again. Finally:

                    LISE (O.C.)
          Oui... je viens.

Billy turns and disappears down the stairs.

EXT. PARIS STREETS - DAY (MOS)

WE HEAR Beethoven's Serenade in D, Opus 41.

Billy is riding in the back seat of a convertible. ERIC,
his cinematographer, is seated next to him. In the front
are a DRIVER and an assistant, CHRISTINE.

Billy is busy, all energy, as he directs the driving,
pointing out shots to Eric, and barking notes to Christine.

Billy taps the driver to pull over. He jumps out of the car
and runs into a cafe.

INT. CAFE

Billy is at a phone, dialing a number.

                    BILLY
          Lucy? It's me, Billy. Any
          messages? Lise didn't call?
          Strange. No... I'm just curious.
          Tell Frank... tell him 'hello'.

He's about to leave. Stops. Dials another number. While
it rings, he searches his rucksack for the telephone beeper.
He puts it to the mouthpiece and presses the button. We can
faintly hear THREE SHORT BEEPS which indicate that there are
no messages on Lise's answering machine.

EXT. QUAI DES GRANDS AUGUSTINS

The car is parked. Billy and Eric are discussing a shot,
using his viewfinder. Eric points to a spot farther away.

                    BILLY
                (to Christine)
          Call the office. Ask Lucy if
          there are any messages for me.

EXT. POMPIDOU CENTER - DAY

Billy, Eric, and Christine are riding the escalators to the
top story. Billy is framing a shot with his hands, using
Christine as a stand-in. Christine is enjoying this, taking
the opportunity to mimic and make fun of 'model'-type poses.

They reach the landing. All of Paris stretches out below
them. The three of them take in the view.

Billy breaks the silence.

                    BILLY
          Would you mind?

Christine holds out her hand. Billy digs into his pocket
and hands her some change. She trundles off.

                    BILLY
                (continuing)
          Sometimes I wish I could go
          someplace where there aren't any
          phones. You know what I mean?

EXT. BOIS DE BOLOGNE - DAY

Lunch. The car is parked. Billy, Eric, and the driver are
eating sandwiches, drinking beer. Christine approaches,
carrying a piece of paper. Billy sees her. He gets up and
runs towards her.

                    BILLY
          What?

                    CHRISTINE
          Three.
               (reading)
          Sophie. Not important. A Mister
          Pitkin. Left a number and will
          call again. American. And Isobel
          Fournier.

                    BILLY
          Who?

                    CHRISINE
          She's your flute teacher. I
          didn't know you played the flute.

                    BILLY
          I don't. Yet. That's all?

                    CHRISTINE
          Yes. Yet?

                    BILLY
          No one else called?

                    CHRISTINE
          I swear.

                    BILLY
          After lunch, ask Lucy to make an
          appointment for me for a lesson.
          When you call.

Christine, long suffering, nods.

                    CHRISTINE
          Billy... I'm hungry.

                    BILLY
          Oh. I'm sorry. Eat, eat.

INT. PARIS DISCOTHEQUE - CLUB PRIVEE

Billy is on the phone, looking glum as he hangs up. Behind
him the place is in full swing: beautiful people dancing,
drinking, and having a swell time.

He makes his way to the bar.

Sitting at a table a few yards away from the bar are Frank,
Mel, Jack, and Paul. They are sharing a bottle of expensive
champagne.

Billy waves to them that he will be over in a minute, but first:

                    BILLY
               (to the bartender)
          Henri, could I have a Coke? And
          some change for the phone.

                    HENRI
          Classique? Nouvelle? Diet?

                    BILLY
          It doesn't matter. Put some rum
          in it.

Henri pours him the drink.

A large, florid, energetic, middle-aged American steps up to
Billy. His name is ARNIE PITKIN.

                    PITKIN
          Billy Sawyer?

                    BILLY
          Maybe. Who wants to know?

                    PITKIN
          Arnie Pitkin. That's who.

                    BILLY
          I'm Billy Sawyer. How do you do?

                    PITKIN
          Wonderful to meet you finally.
          Can I buy you a drink?

                    BILLY
          I have one. State your business,
          Pitkin. You've been hounding me
          for days. What is it?

                    PITKIN
          Simple. You're a director. I'm a
          producer.
                    (produces a large
                     manila envelope)
          I have a script. Read it and, in
          the words of Samuel Goldwyn, tell
          me how you love it.

                    BILLY
          I make commercials, Arnie. This
          looks longer than thirty seconds.

                    PITKIN
          You wanna do that shit all your
          life? No offense. This is a
          feature film. My card's inside.
          Call me. Nice meeting you.

He saunters off.

                    BILLY
                    (to Henri)
          Pitkin... Pitkin. It's a familiar
          name. Do I know this guy?

Billy turns back to the table. He tosses the script down.

                    BILLY
                    (to Frank)
          You know what's weird? I sent her
          five hundred francs worth of
          flowers and she didn't even thank
          me.

                    FRANK
                    (to Billy)
          No. That's not weird. What is
          weird is that you sent them.

                    BILLY
          I'd better call her.

                    FRANK
          You just called.

                    BILLY
          I'm worried, man.

He stands up. Looks over the dance floor at all the pretty
women.

                    BILLY
          Pitkin... Pitkin... Pitkin County.
          It's where Aspen is. In Colorado.

                    PAUL
          Really?

                    MEL
          Yeah. He's right. Pitkin County.

                    JACK
          What's this about?

                    BILLY
          Be right back.

He turns and makes his way to the phones. WE FOLLOW.

PHONE

Billy dials a number.

                    BILLY
               (into phone)
          Sophie, it's Billy. Have you
          heard from Lise today?
               (lying)
          She was supposed to call me. No
          kidding? That's strange. No,
          don't say anything. Thanks. I'll
          let you know if I hear from her.
          'Bye.

He hangs up and heads for the exit.

                    FRANK
          Billy!

THE TABLE

                    BILLY
          Emergency. Gotta go.

He runs off.

INT. STAIRCASE/LANDING OUTSIDE LISE'S APARTMENT - NIGHT

Billy flies up the stairs leading to Lise's apartment. He stops at the door, panting. He catches his breath, rehearses a smile, and knocks.

WE HEAR the dog barking inside. The door opens slowly and Lise appears, wearing a negligee. She smiles at him. Their eyes lock and they remain silent for a moment, looking amorously at each other.

                    LISE
          I'm so glad you came. I've been
          trying to reach you. The flowers
          were beautiful.

She moves closer, puts her arms around him.

                    LISE
               (continuing)
          You know, I think I made a very
          big mistake.

They kiss passionately. Lise's negligee falls on the floor. Billy's jacket follows. The dog is watching them. He's ecstatic to see them back together. He's wagging his tail against a piece of furniture.

The SOUND of the dog's tail becomes a KNOCK on Lise's door. Billy is knocking on the door. In real life this time. It was just another fantasy.

The dog BARKS again. Lise opens the door. She doesn't seem particularly pleased to see Billy. She's wearing regular clothes.

                    LISE
          What are you doing here?

                    BILLY
          Did you get the flowers?

                    LISE
          Yes, I got the flowers. They were
          beautiful. Thanks. They called
          me for a job this morning and I've
          been running all day. I didn't
          find the time to call you. Sorry.

                    BILLY
     I was worried about you. Sophie
     told me you didn't show up. I
     thought something might have
     happened.

                    LISE
     You called Sophie?

                    BILLY
     I was worried.

                    LISE
     What is this, a police
     investigation?
               (raising her voice)
     You have no right to call my
     friends to spy on me. You have no
     right!

                    BILLY
               (raising his voice, too)
     You're still my wife, damnit!

                    LISE
     I am not!

Lise slams the door on Billy. He walks away a few steps,
hesitates, then goes back to the door and knocks again.

Lise does not answer. Billy walks away.

INT. LISE'S APARTMENT - LATER THAT NIGHT

Lise is coming out of the shower, drying herself. She walks
naked into the living room and freezes as she hears a KNOCK
on the window. She can see a silhouette of a man on the
balcony. She covers herself up, opens a cabinet drawer and
takes out a pistol. Then she recognizes Billy.

                    BILLY
               (muffled sound)
     Let me in!

                    LISE
               (aiming the pistol
                at Billy)
     Go away!

                    BILLY
          I can't!

                    LISE
          Go back the way you came.

She closes the curtains. Billy starts banging on the glass
door.

                    BILLY
                (muffled)
          I can't. I'm stuck. Come on,
          Lise. Let me in.

Out of exasperation, Lise opens the door to the balcony and
lets Billy in. He sees the gun.

                    BILLY
          What's that?

                    LISE
          It's a gun. For shooting people
          who come through windows.

                    BILLY
          Jesus, it's a good thing I said
          something. You could have shot
          me.

                    LISE
          I will if you don't go.

                    BILLY
          What's all the rush about?

Lise goes to the phone and picks up the receiver.

                    LISE
          Because I'm sick and tired of your
          little tricks, that's why! And if
          you don't leave right now, I'm
          going to call the police.

And she means it.

                    BILLY
          It's my apartment, too. I'm
          allowed to be here.

                    LISE
          I knew I should have shot you. I
          would have gotten off, too.

                    BILLY
          I can't believe this. You're
          talking about killing me. Lise,
          do you think we've grown apart?
          Just kidding. Seriously... let's
          just talk this out.

                    LISE
          I don't want to talk. Not now.
          I'm tired.

                    BILLY
          When, then? Tomorrow?

                    LISE
          Not tomorrow and not the day
          after. I know what you have to
          say and I don't want to hear it
          again!

                    BILLY
          You do not know what I have to
          say. And if you shoot me you'll
          never find out. Is that really
          loaded?

                    LISE
          No. All right... what is it?

                    BILLY
               (after a beat)
          I came back to apologize.

                    LISE
          Great. Fine. I accept your
          apologies.

                    BILLY
          Don't you want to know what I'm
          apologizing for?

                    LISE
          I assume everything. And I
          accept. Now, please go.

She goes towards the entrance, but Billy does not budge.

                    BILLY
No, wait! You don't know.
          (a beat)
It's really bad.
          (suddenly dramatic)
Oh, my God, Lise. I'm sorry. I
couldn't help it.

                    LISE
If it's an affair with one of my
friends, I don't want to know.

                    BILLY
Don't be ridiculous. It's worse.
I've been spying on you. I've
been listening to your messages
with my beeper.

                    LISE
That's it?

                    BILLY
No. There's more. I followed you
at Archestrate the other day.

                    LISE
Billy, you're crazy.

                    BILLY
I agree. It's got to stop... and
it's going to stop. No more.
That's it. You live your life,
I'll live mine.

                    LISE
Wonderful. Now I think you should
go.

                    BILLY
But I mean it this time. I swear.
I'm going to leave you alone.
It's all over. And I tell you
what... I think we both should get
a new start, go separate ways--
          (a glimpse at Lise to
           check her reaction)
Maybe new relationships.

                    LISE
You mean it?

                    BILLY
          Swear to God.

                    LISE
          That's great, Billy. I'm glad to
          hear you say that.

                    BILLY
          Are you... do you... I don't think
          we should rush into anything, do you?

                    LISE
          I think we'll be happier that way.

Billy did not expect this reaction from Lise. He is caught
off balance. Trying to save face, he goes to a cabinet and
takes out a bottle of whisky and two glasses.

                    BILLY
          Great... great. This is great.

                    LISE
          What are you doing?

                    BILLY
          We've got to drink to that. Let's
          celebrate.
                    (pours whisky and
                    hands Lise a glass)
          To new lives! To friendship!
          Don't you want a drink?

                    LISE
          I'm sorry, Billy, but I had a very
          hard day. I have to go to bed.

                    BILLY
          Absolutely. It's okay. The
          important thing is that you and I--

                    LISE
          Please... no more.

                    BILLY
          Okay. Yes, okay. I'm sorry.

He puts her glass down and drinks his in one gulp.

                    BILLY
               (continuing)
          Well--

                    LISE
          Good night, Billy.

She leads him towards the entrance. He turns around and
looks at his flowers that are displayed all over the
apartment.

                    BILLY
          Nice flowers.

                    LISE
          Thank you. They really are
          gorgeous.

                    BILLY
          You're welcome.

They have reached the door. There is a pause.

                    BILLY
          Oh, by the way. They're screening
          my film at the Cinematheque
          Friday.

                    LISE
          That's nice, Billy.

                    BILLY
          It would mean a lot to me if you
          could be there.

                    LISE
          Why?

                    BILLY
          It would just be... I mean, you
          were there when I made it. It's
          like... a part of us.

                    LISE
          I don't know, Billy.

                    BILLY
          Well, think about it. If you're
          not busy. You know, we could get
          some dinner afterward.
                    (on her look)
          Or nothing. It would be nice to
          know you were there.

                    LISE
          I can't promise.

                    BILLY
          Sure. Well... good night.

                    LISE
          Good night.

He walks out.

                                        CUT TO:

EXT. STREET - NIGHT

Billy's old Porsche speeding. It passes by a bar, comes to
a screeching halt, then backs up and parks on a pedestrian
crossing.

Billy jumps out of the car and heads towards the bar.

INT. BAR - NIGHT

He walks to the bar.

                    BILLY
          J and B, s'il vous plaît.

In the room, all the tables are occupied. Billy looks
around, checking out the women.

The bartender pours Billy's J and B. Billy hands him a
bill.

He spots two rather attractive girls who just came in, and
makes his way to them.

GIRL #1 next to him looks at him. He smiles.

                    BILLY
                 (to Girl #1)
          Hi. my name is Billy Sawyer.

Girl #1 doesn't react. GIRL #2 notices him.

                    GIRL #2
          Qu'est-ce-qu'il veut, cui-la?

                    GIRL #1
          Je ne sais pas.

Billy keeps smiling. He holds his hand out.

                    BILLY
          Mon nom... Billy Sawyer.

                    GIRL #2
               (to Billy)
          Get lost.

She puts her arm around Girl #1's waist and gives her a
little kiss on the mouth.

Billy, his arm outstretched, feels like a fool. He grabs
his glass and drinks it down in one gulp.

He looks around the room, ignoring the two girls. At a
table, he notices a WOMAN with a group of friends, who
appears to be looking at him, smiling. Billy smiles back.
They really seem to be hitting it. Only when he turns
around to pick up his glass he realizes that the woman is
smiling at the YOUNGER MAN standing next to him.

Billy finishes his drink and walks out.

EXT. BAR - NIGHT

Billy heads towards his car. He kicks an empty beer can and
sends it rolling out of the blue.

                    WOMAN'S VOICE (O.C.)
          Monsieur! Monsieur!

Billy looks back. Two gorgeous girls (JANICE and LESLIE) in
their late twenties run to him.

                    BILLY
          Moi?

                    JANICE
          Oui.

                    LESLIE
               (in poor French,
                heavy American accent)
          Où est le Rue Bonaparte, s'il vous
          plaît?

                    BILLY
              (phony French accent)
         The Rue Bonaparte.. Oh... it is
         veree far from eere!

                    JANICE
         You speak English?

                    BILLY
         A leetle... I try.

                    LESLIE
         How do we get there?

                    BILLY
              (showing his car)
         Veree easee.

The two girls look at each other. They hesitate.

                    JANICE
         We were going to take the Metro.

                    BILLY
         The Metro? Now? Are vous crazee?
         Tres dangereux pour vous... les
         muggers, les rapists, les assassins...
              (a pause, then,
               with great dignity:)
         I am a gentleman. Vous are safe
         wiz moi.

Billy's sudden formal tone of voice makes the girls laugh.

                    BILLY
         I am Jacques.
              (bows slightly)

                    JANICE
         I'm Janice, and she's Leslie.

EXT. BILLY'S CAR - NIGHT

The Porsche, top down, slaloming in the traffic on the
Champs Elysees.

INT. BILLY'S CAR - NIGHT

Leslie is sitting next to Billy, and Janice is in the back.

They are both excited and a little scared by Billy's
"French" driving style. The radio is blasting. Piaf sings
a love song.

                    JANICE
          Are you sure this is the right
          direction, Jacques? I thought it
          was the other way.

                    BILLY
          I cannot take just any street. I
          take the most beautiful streets
          for vous.
                    (indicating the Champs Elysees)
          Vous do not like?

                    LESLIE
          It's so beautiful...

                    BILLY
          I will show vous Paree by night.

                    JANICE
          We should go back to our hotel--

                    BILLY
          Of course... if you insist. La
          nuit, she is still young.

                    JANICE
          --Maybe smoke some grass first.

                    BILLY
          Ah... See Paree... stoned.
          Magnifique. Fantastique.

                    LESLIE
          Oh, Jacques, you're so French!

                                        CUT TO:

EXT. ARC DE TRIOMPHE - NIGHT

Billy's Porsche speeding around the Arc de Triomphe.
Another Piaf song is heard on the radio: "La Vie En Rose".
The three of them sing with Piaf.

As Piaf's song goes on, WE SEE Billy's car speeding by:

THE EIFFEL TOWER

NOTRE DAME

THE ALEXANDER III BRIDGE

EXT. BRIDGE - NIGHT

Billy, Janice, and Leslie are leaning against the bridge.
Billy, in the middle, has his arms around the girls.

                    JANICE
          God, it's so beautiful.

                    LESLIE
          Everything I ever dreamed about.
          Jesus.

Billy reaches down and brings up a bottle of champagne.

                    BILLY
          Are we happee?

The girls turn to him. Billy kisses Janice, then Leslie.

                    LESLIE
          Say it in French. Say, we're
          happy.

                    BILLY
          Nous sommes joyeux.

                    LESLIE/JANICE
          Nous sommes joyeux.

                    LESLIE
          He is cute.

                    JANICE
          Let's take him back to Tulsa.

                    BILLY
          Tul-sa?

                    LESLIE
          It's in Oklahoma, honey.

                    BILLY
          Oui. Take me to Oklahoma. Take
          me anywhere.

The three of them embrace. Janice and Leslie look at each
other. Billy kisses Janice full on the lips, then Leslie.
Things are about to get out of hand.

                    BILLY
          But first we must make one more
          visit.

                    LESLIE
          Whatever you say, Jacquie. We're
          all yours.

One more group squeeze and another jolt of champagne.

                                        CUT TO:

EXT. LISE'S APARTMENT BUILDING - NIGHT

The car comes to a dead stop in front of the building.

INT. BILLY'S CAR - NIGHT

The girls look around.

                    LESLIE
          Is this place famous?

Billy springs up, clinging to the windshield. He is
wearing his beret and scarf. He is holding the now empty
bottle of champagne, and is obviously drunk. He looks in
the direction of Lise's apartment.

                    BILLY
                 (yelling)
          Lise! Lise! It's me, Billy!

                    JANICE
          Billy?

                    BILLY
                 (yelling)
          You really think I'm sorry, don't
          you? Well, I've got news for you,
          I'm not!

Janice and Leslie look at each other, quite puzzled.

                    BILLY
               (to the girls)
          Be right back.

He leaps out of the car and walks up to the building.

                    BILLY
               (continuing)
          You hear me? I'm not sorry!

                    JANICE
          This guy is definitely not French.

                    LESLIE
          Definitely a creep.

They get out of the car.

                    BILLY
          And I don't give a goddamn what
          you think. That's right. You know
          why? Because I don't need you
          anymore! I'm having a great time
          without you! I'm having a great
          time with my friends here--

He looks into the car and notices that Janice and Leslie are
gone.

                    BILLY
               (continuing)
          --With my friends who were here--
               (looking around)
          Where are they? We're having a
          great time, you hear me? I know
          that you can hear me, but you're
          hiding because you're too scared
          to face the truth!
               (laughing)
          That's it! You're too scared to
          face the truth!

Lights start going on in the buildings around him. People
appear at windows and yell at Billy.

                    VOICE #1 (O.C.)
          Tu la fermes ou j'appelle les
          flics!

                    VOICE #2 (O.C.)
          Va donc cuver ton vin, alcoolique!

EXT. LISE'S APARTMENT BUILDING - NIGHT

The door leading to Lise's balcony opens. Lise appears.

                    LISE
          Will you stop it, Billy? You are
          going to wake up the whole
          neighborhood!

                    BILLY
               (louder)
          I don't care if I wake up the
          whole city, the entire world!
          Nobody is going to stop me from
          telling you what I think about
          you! You want to know what I
          think about you? I think you're
          nuts! You're NUTS!

                    LISE
          You really blew it this time,
          Billy. That's it.

She closes the door and walks away.

                    BILLY
          You're damn right, that's it! And
          you can beg me... you can crawl on
          your knees, nothing is going to
          make me change my mind, you hear
          me? No way, Jose! IT'S OVER!
               (to the people at
                the windows)
          You can go to bed, all of you. the
          show is over.

Billy walks back to the car.

Scrawled on his windshield in lipstick is one word:
"ASSHOLE".

                                        CUT TO:

EXT. PARIS APARTMENT BUILDING - DAY

Billy pulls up, finds a parking spot, gets out. He's
carrying his flute case. He consults an address written on
a piece of paper. He heads for a building and enters.

INT. APARTMENT BUILDING

Billy climbs a couple of flights of stairs. Stops. His
head is hurting from last night's drinking bout. He
continues, finds the door, and rings the bell.

INT. ISOBEL'S APARTMENT - DAY

As the CAMERA EXPLORES ths apartment, WE HEAR a strange
sound. We discover Billy blowing in his flute, trying to
play.

Next to him stands the woman we saw in the Metro playing the
flute in the woodwind ensemble. She is the flute teacher
the salesman in the music store found for Billy. Her name
is ISOBEL.

                    BILLY
          Whhhhh...
               (nothing)

Isobel adjusts the flute.

                    BILLY
          Whhhhh...
               (nothing)
          This is hard.

                    ISOBEL
          Again. Don't breathe too hard.
          Try it gently.

                    BILLY
               (nothing; frustrated now;
                tries harder and harder)
          Damn!

                    ISOBEL
          Stop. Rest for a moment.

                    BILLY
          I'm sorry.

                    ISOBEL
          Don't worry. It happens all the
          time. But once you get it, it
          becomes very easy.

                    BILLY
          Maybe. My headache--

                    ISOBEL
          Would you like some coffee? Aspirin?

                    BILLY
          Do you mind? I'm not sure if I'm
          ready for this right now.

He follows her into the kitchen.

She pours coffee for them both, and gives him an aspirin.

                    ISOBEL
          May I ask what you do?

                    BILLY
          I'm a director.

                    ISOBEL
          How exciting.

                    BILLY
          Commercials. For TV.

                    ISOBEL
          Oh, I love commercials.

                    BILLY
          Well, I did a feature once. And
          I've just been offered a new
          script. And I'm writing one.

                    ISOBEL
          So busy.

                    BILLY
          Actually, my first film is... will
          be at the Cinematheque. It's--

                    ISOBEL
          Don't tell me. I have the
          schedule.

She consults a schedule tacked to the cupboard door.

                    ISOBEL
          Here... Billy Sawyer. "Manhattan
          Vengeance", nineteen-sixty-six.
          That's you!

                    BILLY
That's me.

                    ISOBEL
Tuesday. May I come?

                    BILLY
Sure.

                    ISOBEL
I have a famous student.

                    BILLY
Busy, not famous.

                    ISOBEL
You seem preoccupied. A bit sad.

                    BILLY
I don't know. Maybe this isn't a
good time to start learning the
flute. I mean, it's something you
have to concentrate on. My wife
and I are going through this
separation and... it's very
boring. I mean, we're
separated... Do you want to hear
all this?

Isobel nods. Billy thinks, is about to continue, then:

                    BILLY
That's it.

                    ISOBEL
I see.

                    BILLY
Well, it's just that flute
lessons-- I mean, playing the
flute seemed to be a good idea...
but I don't seem to be very good
at it, anyway.

                    ISOBEL
Why don't we make another
appointment and you practice a bit
in the meantime. Experiment until
you can make a sound.

                    BILLY
          I just have to relax, right?

                    ISOBEL
          Yes.

                    BILLY
          I'm trying too hard, my first
          lesson.

                    ISOBEL
          Yes.

                    BILLY
          It's like sex. You try too hard,
          nothing happens.

                    ISOBEL
          You can't get it up.

                    BILLY
          What?

                    ISOBEL
          Isn't that the expression?

                    BILLY
          Sort of. How much... for the
          lesson?

                    ISOBEL
          Nothing today. We'll start next
          time.

                    BILLY
          No, I insist.

                    ISOBEL
          No... I insist.

                    BILLY
          You're very kind.

They walk out of the kitchen to the living room. As he puts
his flute back in its case:

                    BILLY
          I didn't mean to drop all that
          stuff on you... personal stuff.

                    ISOBEL
          It's good for you to play the
          flute. You'll see. Come in one
          week. Same time.

At the door:

                    BILLY
          Yes. That's fine. One week.

He steps out. She closes the door.

INT. HALLWAY

Billy walks towards the stairs.

EXT. BUILDING - DAY

Billy comes out of the building carrying his flute case. He
walks to his car, is about to get in, then stops. He opens
his flute case on the roof of the car, assembles it quickly,
puts it to his lips and... a sound. Again... another!

He spins around and races back to the entrance.

INT. BUILDING - STAIRS

Billy bounding up the stairs.

INT. HALLWAY

Billy running down the hallway. Knocks on Isobel's door.

DOOR

Isobel opens the door.

BILLY

At the door.

                    BILLY
          I did it! Watch! I mean, listen!

He blows. Nothing. He tries again. Nothing. He is
despondent.

Isobel adjusts the flute under his lip a quarter turn. He
tries again. Sound. Music. Beauty.

> BILLY
>
> I got it up.

Isobel laughs.

CUT TO:

EXT. CINEMATHEQUE - NIGHT

A poster announces Billy Sawyer's "Manhattan Vengeance".

INT. CINEMATHEQUE AUDITORIUM

WE SEE the end of the film, a black-and-white 'film noir',
the hero shot dead, sliding downward into a rain-soaked
gutter.

AUDIENCE

Isobel sitting off in the corner, applauding when it's over.
We also see Pitkin and Sophie.

A young woman ANNOUNCER waits by the side of the screen to
introduce Billy.

> ANNOUNCER
> (in French)
> [It pleases me very much to
> introduce you to the director of
> this evening's film, Billy
> Sawyer--]

Billy steps out of the front row of the audience, to APPLAUSE,
goes up on the stage next to the announcer. He's still
looking for Lise.

> ANNOUNCER
> (to Billy)
> I will translate questions if they
> are in French, and your answers,
> all right?

> BILLY
> I'm sorry, what? Oh... yes.

A member of the audience immediately begins asking a
question in French.

                    QUESTION ASKER #1
                (in French)
          Clearly your work is influenced
          by such directors as Frank, Mekas,
          and Anger, yet you seem to
          repudiate them by having your hero
          die in front of a theatre which is
          playing "Cleopatra". Is that a
          rejection of your avant-garde
          roots in favor of a Hollywood career?

The Announcer translates.

                    BILLY
          Huh? "Cleopatra"... that's what
          was playing there that night.

                    QUESTION ASKER #2
                (in French)
          How do you feel about returning
          to America after you were forced
          into exile. Do you see
          Hollywood's rejection as typical
          of the political filmmaker?

                    BILLY
          I wasn't forced into exile. I
          came here because I wanted to live
          and work in Paris. I can go back
          anytime I want.

A beautiful, dark young woman dressed in a black cape
stands. Her name is ROBIN.

                    ROBIN
          I'm American. I saw "Manhattan
          Vengeance" and to me and people I
          know it was the most important
          film we ever saw. It made us
          question everything, reject
          corrupt values... it changed our
          lives. For me personally it was
          my first -- and to this day, most
          -- intense experience of film art,
          and I just had to take this
          opportunity to lay myself at the
          altar of your genius.

                    BILLY
              (brightens considerably,
               as who wouldn't)
          No kidding.

Robin sweeps her cape around her. People applaud.

INT. CAFE RECEPTION - LATER

The crowd from the Cinematheque is there in this little
party. Among them is Pitkin, Sophie, and Robin. Isobel is
not there.

Billy is surrounded by fans, but Pitkin is overbearing and
Robin, still hanging charged lightning bolts of eye contact,
is across the room. Billy moves to go to her.

But Pitkin stops him.

                    PITKIN
          Billy, delighted to be here, kid.
          The film was brilliant. Not
          really my kind of stuff, but
          brilliant. Genius. Sheer genius.
          Like the girl said, you affected a
          whole generation.

                    BILLY
              (looking over at Robin)
          You know her?

                    PITKIN
          No. So what about the script?
          Did you get a chance to read it?

                    BILLY
          I can't find it. I've been trying
          to get in touch with you for
          another copy.

                    PITKIN
          No problem.

Pitkin just happens to have one in his French briefcase. As
he gives a script to Billy, WE SEE Robin slip out a side
door.

                    BILLY
          Wait--

Billy rushes after her but she is gone.

Billy stands there, looking nonplussed. Sophie approaches.

> SOPHIE
> Billy, it was wonderful. You
> should make another... and another.

> PITKIN
> He's already considering.

> BILLY
> Look, who was that girl? The one
> in the cape? Do you know her?

Pitkin, nearby, is all ears.

> SOPHIE
> She's a fan, for one thing. Stay
> away from fans.

> BILLY
> I just wanted to talk to her. She
> sounded very interesting.

> PITKIN
> You sound lonely, kid.

> BILLY
> I am not lonely. I just found her
> very--

> PITKIN
> I'll take care of it. Read the script.

He walks off. Sophie looks at Billy. "Who is that guy?"

> CUT TO:

INT. ISOBEL'S APARTMENT - DAY

Billy is struggling enthusiastically with the flute. He is
managing to squeak out a few notes and negotiate the basic
fingerings. He and Isobel are justifiably pleased with his
progress.

> BILLY
> (lowering the flute)
> Why didn't you come over, say
> hello?

                    ISOBEL
          You looked so busy. Surrounded by
          all those people.

                    BILLY
          Did you notice the woman who asked
          the question in English... with
          the cape? American.

                    ISOBEL
          Yes. She was very beautiful.
          Strange.

                    BILLY
          You don't know who she is, do you?

                    ISOBEL
          No.

                    BILLY
          I'd really like to find her. Talk
          to her. She had some very
          interesting insights about the
          film.

                    ISOBEL
          Maybe you should put an ad in
          Passion.

                    BILLY
          Passion?

                    ISOBEL
          You know, the magazine. It could
          say, "American director seeks
          American beauty who wishes to lay
          herself on the altar of his genius."

                    BILLY
          As I said, she had some very
          interesting insights about the
          film.

                    ISOBEL
          Play.

INT. COMMERCIAL STUDIO

Frank and the three American advertising guys are crowded
around Billy.

Behind them is a set for the lipstick commercial shoot.
The crew, including ERIC, is preparing the next shot. The
Americans are holding a bag of cookies in front of Billy.
Frank is torn between schmoozing a new assignment and going
overtime on the one he's doing now.

                    PAUL
          Try the chocolate raisin.

                    BILLY
          I did.

                    JACK
          What do you notice most about
          them?

                    BILLY
          That they're crispy on the outside
          and soft on the inside. You think
          I'm a jerk? I can read the box.
          Like home baked.

                    PAUL
          You know what a breakthrough that
          was in baking?

                    MEL
          The guy should get a fucking Nobel
          Prize. He revolutionized cookies,
          let's face it.

                    BILLY
          Great! I'll have every French
          man, woman, and child eating this
          stuff.

                    MEL
          No.

                    BILLY
          No?

                    JACK
          It's for the Germans.

                    BILLY
          I thought the war was over... Just
          kidding.

                    ERIC
          We're ready, Billy.

                    BILLY
          Coming.

He takes a couple of steps towards the camera, then comes
back.

                    BILLY
                 (continuing)
          Wait, you guys know a lot of
          Americans in Paris, right? You
          know a girl, maybe late twenties,
          very beautiful, black hair...
          wears a cape?

There are a lot of blank stares and insincere looks of
interest.

                    FRANK
          Billy, let's go back to the set,
          yes?

                    BILLY
          Okay, time to direct. Eric, do
          you like this shot?

                    ERIC
          I love this shot.

                    BILLY
                 (looks through the
                  viewfinder)
          Beautiful!

Everyone moves into place, including STACEY DOYLE. Her
makeup is adjusted.

Christine enters the room. Billy notices her, motions her
to him. She seems reluctant to approach. Billy goes to her.

                    BILLY
          What is it?

                    CHRISTINE
          Arnie Pitkin called. He said he's
          at the Coupole. He found her...
          the woman in the cape.

                    BILLY
               (softly)
          He found her? She's with him?
               (stepping back; loud now)
          Omigod! I gotta go!

                    FRANK
          Billy. What's the matter?

                    BILLY
          Annie! She got hit by a car!

                    FRANK
          Annie?

                    BILLY
          My sister. She just got here.
          Can you believe it? Her first day
          in Paris. I gotta go.

Frank steps forward to get the message from Christine, but
Billy grabs it first.

                    BILLY
          I'll call you from the hospital.

He dashes off.

                                        CUT TO:

EXT. LA COUPOLE - DAY

Billy heading across the street towards the cafe.

BILLY'S POV

Pitkin rising up out of his chair, waving at him. Seated at
the table, a woman with long black hair, her back to Billy.

Billy slows, adjusts his clothes, approaches nonchalantly.
As he reaches Pitkin's table:

                    PITKIN
          Billy. What a surprise. I was
          just discussing your film with one
          of your biggest admirers.

                    BILLY
                 (super cool)
        Hi. How're you doing?

The girl turns. She can be beautiful, but she can't be the
one who asked the question at the Cinematheque. Her name is
LAURA GRIFF.

                    LAURA
        Fine. Nice to meet you.

                    BILLY
        It's not her.

                    PITKIN
        Say hello to Laura Griff.

                    LAURA
        What do you mean, it's not me?

                    PITKIN
        She's American.

                    BILLY
        Doesn't matter. It's not her.

                    PITKIN
        So at least sit down.

                    LAURA
        Arnie, what is this?

                    PITKIN
        It's nothing. Billy Sawyer, a
        very talented director who is
        reading a script of mine... say
        hello to Laura Griff, a brilliant
        actress. You should know each other.

                    BILLY
        I'm sorry, you may be here under
        false pretenses.

                    LAURA
        False pretenses? What do you
        direct, pornos?

                    BILLY
        It was nice meeting you. I gotta
        go. He thought you were somebody else.
                 (getting up)

                    LAURA
          How could he think I'm somebody
          else? He knows me.

                    PITKIN
          Gimme a minute. I'll explain.

He rushes after Billy and catches up to him.

                    PITKIN
          We'll keep looking. I thought...
          she wears a cape sometimes. I
          swear.

                    BILLY
          Thanks. I appreciate it. But it
          wasn't her. Tell her I'm sorry,
          okay?

                    PITKIN
          No problem. She's a great kid.
          Swell actress. She worked with
          Fellini. I see her as Cleo, what
          do you think?

Billy looks somewhat blank.

                    PITKIN
          You didn't read it yet?

                    BILLY
          I've been really busy. I'll get
          to it this weekend.

                    PITKIN
          Read the script. I know you're
          going to love it.

                    BILLY
          I've gotta go.

Billy leaves.

                    PITKIN
          Hey! You want me to try again?

But Billy is gone.

INT. BILLY'S APARTMENT

He's trying to make sounds with his flute, and change
notes, fooling around. He manages to sort of play "Frère
Jacques".

SFX: PHONE RINGS

                    BILLY
                 (picking up)
          Hello. Speak English, please.

                    SOPHIE
          She's a photographer. She's here
          for her show. Galerie Nicole. In
          the First.

                    BILLY
          That's great. Fantastic. I love
          you.

EXT. PARIS STREET - NIGHT

Billy gets out of a taxi in a small street, and heads for an
art gallery.

INT. ART GALLERY

Billy enters. Looks at the photos on the walls.

PHOTOS

They are black and white studies of morbidity. Charnel
houses, dead animals squashed on southern highways, flooded
villages in Central America. And a self-portrait of the
object of his search. Beauty in a black cape staring at death.

BILLY

Overjoyed. He removes the picture from the wall and takes
it over to the desk.

EXT. GALLERY - NIGHT

Billy steps out, carrying the wrapped picture under his arm,
and an address in his hand. He sets out down the street.

As he waits to cross the next street he looks up.

BILLY'S POV

He sees a billboard of Lise staring at him.

BILLY

He smiles back. He's in good shape. He's in love.

EXT. HOTEL - NIGHT

Billy walks along a small street, checking the numbers on
the buildings. He stops in front of an old, charming hotel
and walks in.

INT. HOTEL

He can be seen addressing the reception clerk. The man does
not seem to understand him. Billy shows him the large
photograph of Robin. Then the man gives Billy Robin's room
number.

INT. HOTEL CORRIDOR - NIGHT

Billy has a hard time finding Robin's room in the dark
corridor.

He finally finds it. Stops. Takes a deep breath.

Before he even knocks, the door slowly opens, without a
sound. It is Robin, all dressed in black. More beautiful
and mysterious than ever. Their eyes lock immediately. A
magical moment. They do not say a word.

Robin slowly walks back into the room, inviting him to come
in. He follows her. They seem to be moving in slow motion.

INT. ROBIN'S ROOM - NIGHT

Billy closes the door behind him. The room is dark. He
notices a poster of his film, "Manhattan Revenge", on the
wall.

They keep staring at each other. They speak in low voices
as he slowly moves closer and closer to her.

                    BILLY
You are so beautiful.

                    ROBIN
You are so talented.

                    BILLY
I've been looking for you all over
Paris.

                    ROBIN
I knew you were coming.

                    BILLY
I've never stopped thinking about
you since that night.

                    ROBIN
I've been waiting for this very
moment for the last fifteen
years--

                    BILLY
Really?

                    ROBIN
--since I saw your film for the
first time in Omaha... January
twenty-second, nineteen seventy-
five.

                    BILLY
          (touched)
You remember...

                    ROBIN
It gave a meaning to my life.

                    BILLY
You are a goddess.

                    ROBIN
You are a genius.

                    BILLY
I need you.

                    ROBIN
I want you.

                    BILLY
     I love you.

                    ROBIN
     I adore you.

                    BILLY
     Forever.

                    ROBIN
     Forever.

Now they are only inches from each other. Their lips meet.

                    ROBIN
               (continuing)
     I want to make love to you.

                    BILLY
     Yes.

                    ROBIN
     I have wanted to make love to you
     since January twenty-second,
     nineteen seventy-five. I want to
     give myself to you in a way that I
     have never given myself to any
     man... completely.

                    BILLY
     I want that.
          (reaching for her)

                    ROBIN
     I want it to be perfect.

                    BILLY
     It will be.

                    ROBIN
     Not here.

                    BILLY
     Of course.
          (pause)
     Why not here?

                    ROBIN
     It's not perfect.

                                        CUT TO:

INT. BILLY'S APARTMENT - DAY

Robin steps in, followed by Billy.

She walks around the apartment as Billy watches her, waiting
for her reaction. She stops in the middle of the room.

                    ROBIN
          No.

                    BILLY
          No?

                    ROBIN
          Too much white light.

                    BILLY
          Well... we can pull down the shades.

                    ROBIN
          Even if we cannot see it, it will
          be there.

Billy looks puzzled.

                    BILLY
          Too much white light?

                    ROBIN
          We must go to the land of the black
          mountains.

                    BILLY
          Where is that?

                    ROBIN
          Longwy.

                    BILLY
          Longwy? You mean in Lorraine?
          Isn't it kind of an industrial region?

                    ROBIN
               (reciting)
          Black mountains of coal on the
          flat land, like breasts of African
          goddesses buried forever.

                    BILLY
          Okay. Let's go there.
                                        CUT TO:

INT. BILLY'S APARTMENT - LATER

Billy's ANSWERING MACHINE rolling. Billy's RECORDED VOICE
is heard.

                    BILLY (FILTER)
          Billy Sawyer is gone. Gone on his
          honeymoon in the land of the black
          mountains. Only messages of
          congratulations are accepted.

SFX: BEEP.

Billy and Robin are walking out. Billy carries a travel bag.

Then WE HEAR Lise's voice on the machine. She sounds sad.

                    LISE (FILTER)
          Well... this sure is a surprise.
                    (pause)
          Congratulations.
                    (then:)
          I think we should talk before you
          go on your honeymoon, though... as
          soon as possible, okay?

Billy stops for a second.

                    ROBIN
          Aren't you going to call her back?

                    BILLY
          No, no... it's just my former wife.

                    ROBIN
          I want to meet her. I want to
          know her. Can we all be friends?

INT. BILLY'S CAR - DUSK

They're moving along the Autoroute de l'est. Billy is at
the wheel, Robin is sitting next to him. Gregorian chants
are heard on the cassette player.

                    BILLY
          You know, you really inspire me.
          I feel this is the beginning of a
          whole new phase in my life. I
          just decided I'm going to make
          another picture.

                    ROBIN
          You're going to make another film?

                    BILLY
          Yes!

                    ROBIN
          Why?

                    BILLY
          What do you mean?

                    ROBIN
          You've already made your
          masterpiece.

Billy looks puzzled.

                    ROBIN
                 (continuing)
          Do you know Matteo Taverna?

                    BILLY
          Matteo Taverna? I don't think so.

                    ROBIN
          He is the greatest novelist who
          ever lived. Your equivalent in
          literature. He wrote one book --
          a masterpiece, and then he shot
          himself.

Billy looks worried.

                    ROBIN
                 (continuing)
          I agree with Camus. There are
          only three solutions for the
          existential man... crime, suicide,
          or madness.

EXT. BILLY'S CAR - DUSK

The car can be seen moving rapidly along an off-ramp and
stopping by a gas station.

INT. BILLY'S CAR - DUSK

                    BILLY
          I'll be right back.

Billy gets out of the car.

INT. PHONE BOOTH - DUSK

Billy is on the phone.

                    BILLY
          Hello, Lise? You want to talk? I
          haven't left yet. I could be
          there in half an hour. I'm just
          around the corner. No, it's okay.
          All right... I'll be there at nine.

Billy hangs up. Now he has a problem.

EXT. GAS STATION - DUSK

Billy exits the phone booth. Robin is chatting with GERALD,
a young American back-packer.

                    ROBIN
          Billy, you must meet Gerald.

                    BILLY
          How do you do?

                    ROBIN
          He's a poet. I told him all about
          us. He's such a beautiful poet...
          I want him to come with us to
          Longwy. The three of us.

                    BILLY
          I'm sorry, Robin... I have some
          very bad news. Thank God I called
          my service.

                    ROBIN
          Billy--

                    BILLY
          It was a call from my agent. They
          want me in Hollywood.

                    ROBIN
          Hollywood?

                    BILLY
          They want me to direct a movie.

                    ROBIN
          Oh, Billy... no.

                    BILLY
          Rambo Five.

                    GERALD
          Rambo Five... that sucks, man.

                    BILLY
          The poet speaks. Robin, I must go
          back to Paris.

She looks at Gerald.

                    ROBIN
          I can't go with you to Hollywood,
          Billy. You know that.

                    BILLY
          Than go to Longwy. Go... with
          Gerald. Will you think of me as
          the man who made one film before
          he died a commercial death in
          Hollywood, impaled on the cross of
          Rambo?

She nods sadly and embraces him farewell.

                                        CUT TO:

INT. BILLY'S CAR - NIGHT

Billy pulls out of the gas station, heading back towards
Paris.

In the REAR VIEW MIRROR:

Gerald and Robin hitchhiking.

                                        CUT TO:

INT. NEIGHBORHOOD CAFE - NIGHT

Lise is sitting in the corner when Billy comes into the cafe.

Lise is wearing old jeans, a sweater, and is generally not in one of her knock-out get-ups. Billy sits down.

                    BILLY
          It's good to see you.

Lise is all business.

                    LISE
          Okay. Let's talk about it.

                    BILLY
          About what?

                    LISE
          The divorce.

                    BILLY
          A divorce? Why?

                    LISE
          You left a message on your machine
          about a honeymoon. I suppose you
          want to get married. It's fine
          with me. I just think we should
          get divorced first.

                    BILLY
          That was a joke.

                    LISE
          Not funny.

                    BILLY
          I can't believe I just drove two
          hours, endangering my life, to
          come here and talk to you about
          divorce.

                    LISE
          Two hours? You said you were
          around the corner. Can't you ever
          tell the truth? God, I can't
          understand you. I never did and I
          never will. Look, you're just
          going to have to accept this.
          We're getting divorced.

                         BILLY
          No we're not! You're getting
          divorced. I'm not doing anything.
          I won't have anything to do with
          this.

                         LISE
                    (getting up)
          You make me so crazy. You talk to
          my lawyer.

Lise shrugs and exits.

                         BILLY
                (at the top of his voice)
          I'm not talking to anybody!

EXT. STREET - LATER THAT SAME NIGHT

Billy is wandering aimlessly. He comes to a movie theatre
and pays to go in.

INT. MOVIE THEATRE - NIGHT

Billy sits down in an audience that is rolling with
laughter. Billy is not laughing. The more the audience
laughs, the more sullen Billy becomes.

Finally the movie ends. People, limp with laughter, begin
to leave. Billy sits still, and a commercial comes on the
screen.

It's a PORSCHE COMMERCIAL. A gorgeous blonde is driving a
Porsche while an incredibly handsome young man in black
leather rides a motorcycle beside her, flirting
outrageously, obviously making an assignation to meet. WE
SEE that the blonde is Lise.

Billy begins trembling with anger and leaps to his feet.

                         BILLY
              No, no, no!!

Billy stomps out of the theatre.

EXT. BILLY'S BUILDING - DAY

Billy frantically packing things into his car.

EXT. LISE'S BUILDING - DAY

Billy is sitting in his car, watching Lise's building.

She comes out.

Billy watches as she gets into her car and speeds away.

INT. LISE'S APARTMENT - NIGHT

DOOR

It opens, and Lise enters.

LISE

She looks around, surprised.

LISE'S POV

The table is elegantly set for two. Flowers, candles, good
crystal, an expensive bottle of wine in a wicker basket.

Billy stands beside his chair.

                    BILLY
          Lise, we tried it your way -- this
          separation -- it didn't work. Now
          we're going to try it my way. I
          made dinner.

Lise looks at him for a moment, this madman. In addition,
she's had a lousy day. She smiles, takes off her coat, and
sits down.

                    BILLY
               (pours her some wine)
          So, how was your day?

                    LISE
               (takes a swallow)
          Very busy. I had an early
          session. Miriam Sophie was the
          photographer. You remember her,
          she did some stills for you once--

                                        CUT TO:

DINNER TABLE - LATER

Billy is offering Lise a second cup of coffee. She declines.

                    BILLY
          There's a lot I'm willing to
          change. Or at least talk about.
          I plan to stay home a lot. I'll
          work on my screenplay. You can...
          read. But we're definitely
          cutting down on our superficial
          social life.

                    LISE
          Excuse me just a minute.

She gets up and goes into the bedroom as Billy continues:

                    BILLY
          And as far as friends are
          concerned, from now on, either we
          both like them, or we drop them.
          No more inflicting people we're
          uncomfortable with on each other.
          And that goes for relations, too.
          Yours and mine. Okay... mostly
          mine.

Lise enters. She is carrying a suitcase.

                    LISE
          Thanks for dinner, Billy. It was
          lovely.

                    BILLY
               (standing)
          Where are you going?

                    LISE
          Home.

                    BILLY
          This is home. Home is here.

                    LISE
          No. Home is where you're not.

She leaves. And leaves Billy desolate.

                                   CUT TO:

INT. RUSSIAN BATHS

Frank and Billy are in the wet steam room. Billy is lying on
his stomach while a huge MASSEUSE is swabbing his body with
eucalyptus leaves. Between strokes Billy manages to say:

                    BILLY
          It was working. She was going
          with it. And then I said
          something wrong. Impulsive...
          that's me. It's my personality.
          At one point she found it very
          attractive.

From Frank's expression we might gather that Billy has been
going on for a long time.

                    BILLY
                (continuing)
          I can't stand being in the
          apartment without Lise. There are
          just too many reminders of her.
          You see, I thought if I left at
          least I would know where she is.
          Now I don't know where she is, or
          who she's with. It is really
          starting to drive me crazy. What
          do you think?

The masseuse pours a bucket of ice water over Billy,
interrupting him momentarily.

INT. SHOWER

Billy and Frank are showering.

                    BILLY
          I was thinking of writing to Lise.
          A long letter, putting down all my
          thoughts, explaining things in a
          calm way. You know, whenever we
          get together we fight... so maybe
          a letter. What do you think?

INT. LOCKER ROOM

Billy and Frank are dressing.

                    BILLY
          Secretly, I think she still loves
          me. There's just a lot of anger
          she's not dealing with. It may
          not even have anything to do with
          me. It could be about her career,
          her childhood. What do you think?

Frank takes a deep breath and tells him.

                    FRANK
          I think you are boring the shit
          out of me. And I will tell you
          what else I think. You don't care
          about anybody or anything except
          yourself and your problems. There
          are people starving to death,
          people whose buildings are falling
          on them, people being killed in
          South Africa, millions of tons of
          atomic weapons ready to go off...
          do you care? No. You only see
          yourself. And your friends. I
          tell you, we-- I have had enough.
          Do you say, "How are you, Frank?
          Is everything all right? Are you
          sick? Are you dying? How is it
          now that your wife and children
          are on vacation. Are you lonely?"
          No. You don't say anything except
          Lise, Lise, Lise. Don't ask me
          what I think. I am no longer
          interested.

Billy is speechless. Then:

                    BILLY
          Oh, God. You're right. This is
          terrible, Frank. Will you forgive
          me?

Frank shrugs. He might want to play this a bit longer.

                    BILLY
                  (continuing)
          I've turned into a monster. A
          real creep. Jesus.

Frank warms up a little.

                    FRANK
          Well--

                    BILLY
          I'm really sorry, Frank. Are you
          all right? What's going on with
          you?

                    FRANK
          Well... things are a little rough,
          but--

                    BILLY
          I want to hear all about it. I
          can't believe I've been acting
          this way. And you know why?
          Because I've been under a spell.
          That woman has got me by the balls
          and I let her. That's my fault,
          not hers. So, from this moment
          on, she does not have control
          because I'm not giving it to her.
          Damn, I'm going to tell her, too.
          No, I'll put it in the letter.
          What do you think?

Frank raises his fist at Billy.

                    BILLY
                 (continuing)
          Just kidding. Are you lonely?

                                        CUT TO:

INT. ISOBEL'S APARTMENT - DAY

On something: a tray with two coffee cups, or a picture on
the wall, something. WE HEAR the flute playing long,
beautifully modulated half notes. Billy is under the spell.

ISOBEL AND BILLY

She's playing. He's watching, holding his flute.

                    ISOBEL
          Now you.

Billy plays. Not as sweetly as Isobel, but not bad, either.
Isobel points to a line of music. Billy plays. The notes get
higher and higher. He squeaks out.

                    ISOBEL
          Smile on the high notes.

                    BILLY
          Smile?

She nods. He smiles and produces the tone.

                    ISOBEL
          Lovely. You have talent.
                (points to the music)
          Try it again.

Billy tries. The high notes don't come out this time.

                    ISOBEL
          You're tired.

                    BILLY
          Lesson over?

                    ISOBEL
          Yes.

Billy puts his flute away. Isobel carries the tray into the
kitchen. By the time she returns Billy is ready to leave.
He is counting out the lesson fee.

                    ISOBEL
          Thank you.

                    BILLY
          Thank you.

For some reason, there is an uncomfortable silence.

                    BILLY
                (continuing)
          What now?

                    ISOBEL
          Now?

                    BILLY
          Do you have another student?

                    ISOBEL
          No.

                    BILLY
          What about dinner?

                    ISOBEL
          Me for dinner?

                    BILLY
          Why not?

                                        CUT TO:

INT. NEIGHBORHOOD RESTAURANT - NIGHT

Billy and Isobel are eating at a table by a window. Across
the street is a hand-painted sign advertising the services
of Madame Basquiat, "Voodoo - Problemes d'Amour".

                    BILLY
               (indicating the sign)
          Amazing, isn't it? Somebody can
          actually advertise, make a living
          selling witchcraft. Welcome to
          the twentieth century.

                    ISOBEL
          Should we burn her at the stake?

                    BILLY
          We should just make her put out a
          warning: "This is magic and will
          not work. You are throwing your
          money away."

                    ISOBEL
          But it's for love. "Problems d'
          Amour". You must fight magic with
          magic. You believe love is
          rational?

                    BILLY
          No, it isn't.
               (pause)
          Why isn't it?

Isobel shrugs at this silly question.

                    BILLY
                 (continuing)
          I'm a rational person. I believe
          in science, focal lengths, radar,
          medicine--

                    ISOBEL
          But not voodoo.

                    BILLY
          When you play in public, would you
          rather pray you play well, or
          practice?

                    ISOBEL
          I pray I'll practice well.

                    BILLY
          Okay. I could live with that.

                    ISOBEL
          A compromise.

                    BILLY
          Only because I'm rational.

                                        CUT TO:

EXT. STREET - DAY

Billy comes out of the apartment building with the hand-
painted voodoo sign. He is hiding a package inside his
buttoned jacket. He is about to cross the street when
suddenly he hears a SCREECHING of brakes.

STREET

A huge Cadillac convertible backs up towards Billy. In the
driver's seat is Pitkin, waving, weaving, and yelling.

                    PITKIN
          Billy! Billy!

Billy is trapped. The Cadillac backs up erratically. Billy
jumps out of its path. The package falls out of his jacket
as Pitkin leaps out of the Cadillac, which is parked halfway
on the sidewalk. Its enormous size creates a narrow path
for other cars, honking horns, which Pitkin ignores.

                    PITKIN
          Billy! So! Gimme an answer. Yes
          or no. No! I take that back. A
          'yes' or a 'maybe' is the least
          I'll hear. So?

As Billy picks up the package.

                    PITKIN
                 (continuing)
          Move over here. Something smells.
          Listen, did I tell you I can get
          Bronson? No shit. I can get to
          him. Wait a minute. These people
          are driving me nuts.

Pitkin raises the hood of the Caddie, shrugs helplessly at
the motorists who have to squeeze by.

                    BILLY
          I'm sorry... I just haven't had a
          chance--

                    PITKIN
          I know you're a busy guy. You
          must have a pile of them waiting
          for you. But this one... It's
          real. It's a go. I told you
          about Bronson?
                 (to a taxi)
          Go ahead! You got plenty of room.

                    BILLY
          The thing is, I just moved and all
          my stuff is in boxes. I don't
          know where anything is.

                    PITKIN
          Not to worry. Here.

He reaches into the back seat and comes up with a fresh
script.

                    PITKIN
                 (continuing)
          Listen, read ten, twenty, twenty-
          five pages and if you don't like
          it, that's it. Take it with you
                    (MORE)

                    PITKIN (CONT'D)
          to the can. Also, know that if
          you don't like it, you can rewrite
          it. That's how confident I am of
          your talent.

                    BILLY
          I appreciate that.

At this point Billy and Pitkin are leaning on the Caddie, almost
relaxed. Soft rock and roll MUSIC is coming from the radio:
Temptations.

                    PITKIN
          You all right?

                    BILLY
          I'm fine.

                    PITKIN
          Really?

                    BILLY
          Really.

                    PITKIN
          We're Americans. We have to stick
          together.

                    BILLY
          Right.

                    PITKIN
          You got troubles.

                    BILLY
          Well, things have been a little
          rough--

                    PITKIN
          Did you find that dame?

                    BILLY
          I did, actually.

                    PITKIN
          That was funny, I tried to con you
          with that broad, wasn't it?

                    BILLY
          Yeah.

                    PITKIN
          It'll make a great story. What
          the hell, I took the chance. I
          got balls. Was she worth finding?

                    BILLY
          Yes and no. No. I got a problem.
          I'm still hung up on my wife.

                    PITKIN
          How long were you married?

                    BILLY
          Five years.

                    PITKIN
          That's a long time. She in the
          biz?

Billy points to a wall on which is a poster of Lise.

                    PITKIN
          Wow! No wonder. She's
          beautiful... Jesus.

Pitkin leaps into the Caddie and starts the engine.

                    PITKIN
          Can she act?

                    BILLY
          Lise?
                    (points to the poster)
          Sure.

                    PITKIN
          We'll put her in the movie. She
          can play Cleo. If that doesn't
          get her back... if she doesn't
          fall in love with you... Forget it!

Pitkin pulls out into traffic.

                    PITKIN
          Read!

                                        CUT TO:

INT. BILLY/LISE'S APARTMENT - NIGHT

BEDROOM

Billy opens the package he was carrying. It contains a
voodoo doll which looks vaguely like him. He stuffs it
under the bed.

Billy smoothes down the covers and goes to the door.

DOOR

                    BILLY
          Who is it?

                    LISE
          Lise.

Billy opens the door. Lise and the dog. She has a suitcase.

                    BILLY
          You didn't have to ring.

                    LISE
          Why not?

                    BILLY
          It's your apartment. From now on.
          You move in--
                    (indicates his suitcase
                     on the floor)
          --I move out. We're like the
          seasons. Eternal.

                    LISE
          What smells so funny? But you're
          still in it.

                    BILLY
          I'm leaving. I miss you, Lise. I
          really do. That's the truth.

                    LISE
          I know.

                    BILLY
          And you?

                    LISE
          I do but I'm afraid to tell you.

                    BILLY
          No. Don't be afraid. It's all
          right. I miss you, you miss me.
          We should be together... see?

                    LISE
          Billy, don't start again.

                    BILLY
          All right, all right.

Butch the dog pads in, carrying the voodoo doll between his teet

                    LISE
          What's that? Give me that.

She reaches down to take the doll. Butch moves away.

                    LISE
               (continuing)
          Butch! Come here! That's what
          the smell was.

The dog stops. Lise pries the doll out of his mouth. Holds
it up.

                    LISE
               (continuing)
          Where did this come from?

                    BILLY
          How should I know? Maybe the
          cleaning lady's kid--

                    LISE
          Don't be ridiculous. Ugh... it
          smells awful.

She carries it over to the trash can and dumps it in.

Billy is stymied for a moment, then:

                    BILLY
          I want you to have all the keys.

                    LISE
          It's not necessary.

                    BILLY
          Yes, it is. It'll make things
          clearer. I'll get them.

He steps into the kitchen.

INT. KITCHEN

Reaches into the trash, retrieves the doll.

INT. DINING ROOM

                    BILLY
          I think I left them in the
          bedroom.

INT. BEDROOM

Billy tosses the doll under the bed.

INT. DINING ROOM

                    BILLY
          I had them on me all the time.

Billy hands her a key ring and picks up his suitcase.

                    BILLY
                 (continuing)
          Well... I'd better be going. The
          place is pretty clean. There's
          not much in the fridge.

                    LISE
          It's all right.

                    BILLY
          You'll be all right?

                    LISE
          Yes. I'll be all right.

He goes to the door. Stops. Turns to Lise.

                    BILLY
          Tell me one thing. How would you
          feel about working with Bronson?
          Charles Bronson?

                    LISE
          A commercial?

                    BILLY
          A feature.

                    LISE
          You're kidding. And you're
          directing?

                    BILLY
          I'm serious.

                    LISE
          You're asking me?

                    BILLY
          Yes. Would you work with him?
          And me?

                    LISE
          There's a trick here. What is it?

                    BILLY
          No trick. I'm up for a feature
          with Bronson and you would be very
          good for the lead.

                    LISE
          I don't believe you.

                    BILLY
          What do you mean, you don't
          believe me? I'm not good enough
          to have a feature with Charles
          Bronson? Or I'm not good enough
          to have one with you?

                    LISE
          I don't trust you.

                    BILLY
          Oh, really?
               (goes to the phone)
          I am calling my producer.
               (dials a number)
          Arnie? Billy Sawyer. I'm here
          with Lise. We were just
          discussing the Bronson picture.
               (to Lise)
          He wants to meet you.

                    LISE
Who?

                    BILLY
My producer. Arnie Pitkin. What?
When?
          (to Lise)
He's inviting us to his house in
the country this Saturday.

                    LISE
I don't know. It's all sudden.
Shouldn't I talk to Leon?

                    BILLY
Talk to anyone you want. Look,
it's the movies. Movies are sudden.
          (to Pitkin)
She wants to talk to her agent,
Leon Faure.
          (to Lise)
He knows him.
          (to Pitkin)
I'll let you know. Right.
Thanks.
          (hangs up; to Lise)
What's the matter?

                    LISE
I don't know.

                    BILLY
Hey, strictly professional.
Separate cars if you want. No,
that wouldn't look good. But it's
business. No pleasure. I promise.

                    LISE
I don't know. I'll think about it.

                    BILLY
Check it out. Talk to Leon. The
guy's name is Arnie Pitkin.

                    LISE
          (almost distracted)
Okay... Butch!

The dog pads in again with the doll between its teeth.

                    LISE
                 (continuing)
          Oh, God, this dog. Now it's
          getting into the garbage.

She reaches down and takes the doll, smacking the dog on the
head for good measure.

                    LISE
                 (continuing)
          Bad dog! Bad dog!
                 (to Billy)
          I'm sorry. I have to deal with this.

                    BILLY
          I'm on my way. See you.

As she turns to punish or retrain the dog, or whatever,
Billy scoops up the keys from the table.

                                   CUT TO:

INT. FRANK'S APARTMENT HOUSE DOOR - NIGHT

Billy waiting for the door to open, his suitcase and flute
case at his side. The door opens.

                    FRANK
          Billy, they'll be back in two
          weeks. I can manage.

                    BILLY
          It's not just for you. It'll be
          good for me, too.
                 (walking in)

INT. APARTMENT

Frank takes Billy through the apartment.

                    FRANK
          I guess you can have Annie's room.

INT. ANNIE'S ROOM

A canopied chintz-covered four-poster. The bed is covered
with rows of dolls, all neatly awaiting the return of their
owner.

                    FRANK
          Just put the dolls on... the floor.

                    BILLY
          Sure. No problem. This'll be
          great. We're going to have good
          times. Lots of good talks.

                    FRANK
          You know she has a pet snake.

                    BILLY
          I love snakes. I'm taking you to
          dinner tonight.

Billy puts the flute case on the bed.

                    FRANK
                (warily)
          What's that?

                    BILLY
          A flute.

                    FRANK
          You play it?

                    BILLY
          Yeah, I play it.

                    FRANK
          Loud?

                    BILLY
          Jesus Christ, it's a flute, not an
          electric guitar.

                    FRANK
          Okay, okay. I was thinking about
          the snake. He doesn't like music.

                    BILLY
          Are you crazy? They love flutes.
          It's a part of my new life.
          Music. Discipline. It's like I
          was saying to Lise--

                    FRANK
          Let's eat.

                                        CUT TO:

INT. ISOBEL'S APARTMENT

After a flute lesson.

>   BILLY
>   Would you mind if I used the
>   phone?

>   ISOBEL
>   Not at all. If you want privacy--

>   BILLY
>   No, I'm just calling Lise.

He dials.

>   BILLY
>   (into phone)
>   Lise... Billy. How are you?
>   Fine. About tomorrow. I thought
>   if we left early we might have a
>   chance to talk about the script--
>   Well, I... No, if you don't want
>   to-- I'm not going to say it
>   won't make a difference. The guy
>   wants to meet you. He is the
>   producer. Yes, I want you. If I
>   didn't want you I wouldn't have
>   asked you. Well, technically, I'm
>   not the director yet. All right,
>   all right. I don't make
>   assumptions. You're the one.
>   Right. Goodbye.
>   (to himself)
>   Well, that didn't work.

He hangs up. Isobel is doing her best not to look interested.

>   BILLY
>   She changed her mind. I mean, she
>   never actually said she would go.
>   I was doing her a favor, right?
>   (pause; to Isobel)
>   Would you like to come with me to
>   the country tomorrow?

>   ISOBEL
>   Sure.

>   BILLY
>   It's a date.

                    ISOBEL
          A date? Oh... but I never "date"
          my students. Perhaps it's because
          they're all under ten years old.

                                        CUT TO:

EXT. STREET IN FRONT OF ISOBEL'S APARTMENT - DAY

Billy pulls up in front of Isobel's apartment building. No
place to park. He double-parks, gets out, and dashes inside.

INT. ISOBEL'S BUILDING

Billy rings the bell, then turns and heads back to his car.

EXT. STREET

There is already a traffic jam behind Billy's car. As
people blow their horns, Billy jumps in the car and takes
off around the block. Smack into another traffic jam.

EXT. ISOBEL'S APARTMENT BUILDING

Isobel exits, carrying a large shoulder bag. She looks
around. No Billy.

INT. BILLY'S CAR

Billy blows his horn. Finally the culprit (a man, double-
parked) moves his car. Billy continues to drive around the
block, arriving at Isobel's apartment building.

EXT. ISOBEL'S APARTMENT BUILDING

Billy pulls up. Gets out of the car in time to see Isobel
chatting with MADAME BASQUIAT, a black lady in her forties.
Billy looks suddenly nervous.

                    ISOBEL
          Good morning.

                    BILLY
          Morning.

                    ISOBEL
          Billy, this is Madame Basquiat.

                    MADAME BASQUIAT
               (in French)
          [We already met.]

                         ISOBEL
          Really?

                    MADAME BASQUIAT
               (in French)
          [How are you doing?]

                    BILLY
          Wonderful. Wonderful.
               (hustling Isobel into
                the car)
          Gotta go. We're sort of late.
          Nice seeing you again.
               (rushes over to Madame
                Basquiat; shakes his head;
                then, confidentially:)
          Did you--? Does she--?

                    MADAME BASQUIAT
          I don't tell the lady nothing. Is
          that what you mean?

                    BILLY
          Yes.

                    MADAME BASQUIAT
          I'm like a doctor. My patients'
          business is confidential.
          Absolutement!

                    BILLY
          Wonderful.

                                        CUT TO:

EXT. STREETS OF PARIS - DAY

Billy's car dodging through traffic.

INT. BILLY'S CAR

                    BILLY
          Well, finally on our way. Lovely
          lady. We were going to use some
          of her voodoo props on a shoot.
          Never did, but it was a real
          experience meeting her. You know
          her long?

                    ISOBEL
          I teach Thomas.

                    BILLY
          Thomas?

                    ISOBEL
          Her youngest son.

                    BILLY
          Oh... of course.

                                        CUT TO:

EXT. HIGHWAY - DAY

Billy's car proceeding through the French countryside.

INT. BILLY'S CAR

Isobel is reading the script aloud as Billy drives.

                    ISOBEL
          Interior, Chase Manhattan Bank,
          Paris, Day. Angle on the
          terrorists. Ahmed stands up
          behind the counter. He is about
          to fire his rocket launcher. Cut
          to Lance. He fires one quick
          burst from his Mac-ten. Cut to
          Ahmed falling. Cut to Cleo.
          "Jack, I can't take much more of
          this."
                    (Isobel, to Billy)
          Neither can I, I'm afraid.

                    BILLY
          I can cut that line. Keep going.

                    ISOBEL
          Jack takes her in his arms, is
          about to kiss her. Cut to Ahmed.
          Bloodied, he takes a pistol from
          the dead hand of a comrade-- Dead
          hand?

                    BILLY
          A dead comrade.

                    ISOBEL
          He raises the pistol, takes aim.
          Cut to Jack and Cleo. The bullet
          strikes Cleo. She slips out of
          Jack's embrace. Jack spins and
          fires. Cut to Ahmed falling dead.
          Cut to Jack holding the lifeless
          Cleo. Pull back to reveal the
          destruction. Jack lowers Cleo to
          the floor, closes her eyes, turns
          to camera, fights back tears, then
          stands and walks out of the bank.
          Fade out. The end. Thank God!

Billy doesn't say anything. Finally:

                    BILLY
          It definitely needs a rewrite.

                    ISOBEL
          A rewrite?
                  (holding her nose)
          Ugh!

                                        CUT TO:

EXT. COUNTRY LANE - DAY

The car pulls into an estate road, a cloud of dust rises
behind it.

Ahead, we see the house: a turn of the century stone and
turreted structure set in a grove of ash and chestnut trees.
Behind it are acres of fallow fields and forests. As the
car drives up to the house, Arnie and Laura Griff (the
American Arnie tried to foist on Billy) come out to greet them.

                    PITKIN
                  (of the car)
          Put it anywhere.

Billy parks. He and Isobel get out. Greetings and
introductions are exchanged.

                    LAURA
               (to Isobel)
          You wanna drink? A swim? I'll
          show you--

As she leads Isobel to the house, Arnie takes Billy aside.

                    PITKIN
          It's not her.

                    BILLY
          Not who?

                    PITKIN
          Your wife.

                    BILLY
          No. She's a friend.

                    PITKIN
          I'm not putting her in the movie.

                    BILLY
          She doesn't want to be in the
          movie.

                    PITKIN
          Why not?

                    BILLY
          I don't know. She's not an
          actress.

                    PITKIN
          She's nice, though. You like her?
          What's the matter with me? You
          gotta like her. Otherwise you
          wouldn't have brought her. You
          like lobster?

Pitkin puts his arm around Billy as they walk to the house.

                                        CUT TO:

INT. PITKIN'S STUDY/OFICE - DAY

Billy and Pitkin, each with a drink. Pitkin is showing
Billy his trophies: framed one-sheets from his movie career.
They are in English, French, and Italian. No matter what
the film, they each have a muscular hero clutching either a
spear, sword, or gun in one hand and a big-breasted woman in
a torn shirt, toga, or dress in the other. Between the one-
sheets are framed 8x10s of Arnie with stars. One of them is:

                    PITKIN
          Bronson.

Billy leans in for a closer look.

                    BILLY
          Yup. There he is. Bronson.

                    PITKIN
          And me. Pals. Rome. You know
          how bad he wanted to do
          "Gladiator's Revenge"? But Dino
          had him locked up.

Billy looks out the picture window to the small pool and at
the two women, Isobel and Laura, sunning themselves by the pool.

                    PITKIN
          Not bad, huh? Here, look.

He takes Billy back to the wall and the photos.

                    PITKIN
                 (continuing)
          Me and Lolla. Here's Bardot,
          Maria... she was sixteen then,
          would you believe it? Who knew?
          I think it's why I'm in the
          business, you know? The women.
          You should have brought your wife.
          You put a woman near a movie,
          she'll do anything. So?

                    BILLY
          Why me?
                    PITKIN
          I see your commercials, I wanna go
          out and buy the stuff. You sell
          the product, not yourself. You're
          American, it helps me with my
                    (MORE)

                    PITKIN (CONT'D)
          investors. You'll work cheap. We
          get Bronson, we can have a class
          movie. I need a class movie. Get
          some classier dames. No,
          seriously. She's okay... nice kid.

                    BILLY
          The script needs a lot of work.

                    PITKIN
          So?

                    BILLY
          And I'm working on a project of my
          own... an original.

                    PITKIN
          Bring it to me. It's finished?

                    BILLY
          Not yet. So I have to leave
          myself open... consider my options.

                    PITKIN
          Sure, sure. Jesus. At least you
          read it. You know what it is to
          get a director to read a script
          these days? At least now I can
          talk to Bronson. Whew.
               (raises this glass)
          To us.

                                        CUT TO:

EXT. SWIMMING POOL - DAY

Pitkin and Laura are cavorting in the pool. Billy and
Isobel are sitting, watching. Nothing happening.

                    BILLY
          Would you like to go for a walk?

                    ISOBEL
               (relieved)
          Oh, yes.

They get up.

                    PITKIN
          You guys okay?

                    BILLY
          A walk.

                    PITKIN
          Wherever you like. I rent down to
          the river. From there on you're
          trespassing.

Billy nods. They start off.

EXT. WOODS - DAY

Billy and Isobel walking through the woods.

RIVER

Billy and Isobel, their shoes in hand, wading across the shallows.

WOODS

Then continuing alongside the riverbank. They stop and
admire the view.

                    BILLY
          Shall we go on?

                    ISOBEL
          You go. I'll go back... get ready
          for lunch.

                    BILLY
          I won't be long.

They separate. Billy continues on.

BILLY'S POV: He sees a man sitting on the bank, fishing.

BILLY

Walks up to the MAN.

                    BILLY
          Bonjour.

The man looks up from his fishing and nods. It is CHARLES
BRONSON.

                    BILLY
                (continuing)
        Hey. How're you doin'?

                    BRONSON
        Okay. American?

                    BILLY
        Yeah. Billy Sawyer.

                    BRONSON
        Charlie Bronson.
                (they shake)
        Did you read the Tribune today?

                    BILLY
        Uh-huh.

                    BRONSON
        You didn't notice how Pittsburgh
        did?

                    BRONSON
        They won. Five-four.

                    BRONSON
        Great! I left Paris early, didn't
        get the paper.

                    BILLY
        Arnie know you're here?

                    BRONSON
        Arnie?

                    BILLY
        Pitkin.

                    BRONSON
        Where is he? Is he around here?
        Does he know I'm here? I gotta
        go.

He starts to reel in his line.

                    BILLY
        He's got a place about a half-mile
        upstream.

                    BRONSON
               (relaxes)
     Oh... Listen, do me a favor, will
     you? Don't tell him you saw me,
     okay? I like to fish here on
     weekends... in peace. You know
     what I mean.

                    BILLY
     I thought--

                    BRONSON
     Jesus... Arnie Pitkin.

                    BILLY
     According to him you're warm dear
     close personal friends.

                    BRONSON
     He said that? He's got balls.
     Sawyer, right?

                    BILLY
     Right.

                    BRONSON
     Sounds familiar. You're a
     director.

                    BILLY
     Arnie wants me for a film. With
     you. No chance, right?

                    BRONSON
     You said it.

                    BILLY
     He has a script.

                    BRONSON
     Not yours, I hope.

                    BILLY
     No.

                    BRONSON
     Arnie comes on nice at the
     beginning. He'll respect your
     talent, call you genius. Halfway
     through the film you're an
                    (MORE)

                    BRONSON (CONT'D)
          asshole. He'll fire you and
          finish the film himself. Check
          him out. You'll see.

                    BILLY
          You get a lot of scripts?

                    BRONSON
          Sure. From everybody. What the
          hell? Better than not getting
          them. Remember Polanski? When he
          got busted they made him go to
          Vacaville for sixty days. You
          know Vacaville? You're from New
          York, right? It's a nut house on
          the coast. When he was there he
          was given six scripts. Three from
          guards, two from patients, and one
          from a psychiatrist.

                    BILLY
          Any of them any good?

                    BRONSON
          The best was from one of the
          patients. Unfortunately, it
          turned out to be "Gone With The
          Wind".

He turns back to his fishing.

EXT. PITKIN'S POOL - DAY

Billy approaches. Pitkin and Laura are playing backgammon.
Isobel is reading. They all look up as Billy approaches.

                    PITKIN
          You hungry? We'll eat soon.

                    BILLY
          We have to go.

                    PITKIN
          What about lunch?

                    BILLY
          I'm starting to feel sick. My
          fault for walking in the woods.
                    (sneezes)
          An allergy. I'm going to be a
          mess from here on. Hives.

                    PITKIN
          Hives?

                    BILLY
          I swell up like a balloon.

                    LAURA
          Wow!

                    BILLY
          My lips get like saucers.

                    PITKIN
          Enough... enough...

As Isobel looks on in amazement,

                                        CUT TO:

INT. BILLY'S CAR - DAY

Billy and Isobel, driving in silence. Isobel has her shoes
off, her feet up on the dashboard. Pretty sexy. Billy is
thinking as he drives.

EXT. BILLY'S CAR

The script comes flying out of the window as the car speeds by.

INT. BILLY'S CAR

Billy seems more relaxed. Isobel is stifling a laugh. She
lets it go.

                    BILLY
          What's so funny?

                    ISOBEL
          Lips like saucers.

Billy, laughing, flubs his lips.

EXT. BILLY'S CAR - DAY

It stops at a deserted crossroads. Billy gets out of the
car, walks to the center of the crossroads, closes his eyes,
holds out an arm, points, and spins around. He stops, opens
his eyes, looks at Isobel.

                    ISOBEL
              (gleefully)
          Honfleur!

THE CROSSROAD SIGNS

In Billy's direction, a sign reads "Honfleur - 50 KM".

EXT. HONFLEUR - DAY

Billy's car entering Honfleur, a beautiful fishing port on
the Channel in Normandy.

EXT. HONFLEUR STREET - DAY

Billy parks the car.

WATERFRONT

Billy and Isobel walking.

A CAFE

Billy and Isobel having a drink.

TOWN PARK

Isobel looking at a poster column. She motions Billy over.

POSTER COLUMN

An announcement of a concert.

EXT. TOWN HALL - NIGHT

Billy and Isobel entering with the audience.

INT. TOWN HALL

On stage a chamber orchestra is playing the same enchanted
music Billy heard in the subway.

BILLY AND ISOBEL

Sit, blissfully happy, in the audience.

INT. TOWN HALL - LATER

CLOSEUP on Isobel, listening attentively. CAMERA PULLS BACK
to reveal Billy, asleep on her shoulder.

INT. TOWNHALL - LATER

Lights up, audience gone. A lone porter is sweeping the stage.

AUDIENCE

Billy and Isobel. Billy is still asleep. Billy's hand is
square on her breast. Isobel doesn't seem to mind that.
HOLD on that for a while. Finally, Billy awakens, slowly
realizes what he's got, where he is. He just raises his
head, without moving his hand, enough to meet Isobel's
mouth, and they kiss for a nice long time.

                                        CUT TO:

INT. HOTEL ROOM - NIGHT

The CAMERA PANS the room. Clothes, strewn around a bottle
of champagne in a bucket, two glasses, and an empty pizza
box. The bed and in it, Billy and Isobel, naked and happy.

                    BILLY
          We thought we'd be happy in
          Paris.. New York was too much my
          city. My friends, my
          neighborhoods... my language. So
          we came to Paris. Maybe she just
          wanted to be where the lawyers
          spoke French.

                    ISOBEL
          Were you happy in Paris?

                    BILLY
          Me? I'm happy everywhere.
          Everywhere I'm happy, that is.

                    ISOBEL
          And when you're not?

                    BILLY
          Then I'm nowhere. You know that
          expression? "You're nowhere, man."

                    ISOBEL
          Yes. That's good. I like that.
          Can we get more pizza?

                    BILLY
               (reaching for her)
          Later.

                    ISOBEL
          You promise?

                    BILLY
          I promise.

                                        CUT TO:

INT. HOTEL ROOM - DAY

It's raining. Billy and Isobel sitting up in bed. A fine
view of the water and the rain. Between them is a Walkman.
They each have earphones and are listening, touching under
the blankets. Apparently, for the moment, they can't seem
to get enough of each other.

                                        CUT TO:

EXT. HONFLEUR HARBOR - DAY

Billy and Isobel are having a farewell look at the harbor.

                    BILLY
          Where shall we go next?

                    ISOBEL
          Where?

                    BILLY
          Barcelona, London, Venice... New
          York? You'd love New York.

There's something wrong with this. He tries to correct it.

                    BILLY
                (continuing)
          No, not New York. Someplace we've
          both never been.

                    ISOBEL
          Moscow.

                    BILLY
          Moscow? Why Moscow?

                    ISOBEL
          Why not Moscow?

                    BILLY
          I see. I crumble before your
          logic. Okay. Moscow. When?

                    ISOBEL
          First, Paris.

                    BILLY
          Must we?

                    ISOBEL
          Paris.

They head for the car.

                    BILLY
          I'm serious.
                (takes her in his arms)
          I'm really serious.

On Isobel's look, we:

                                        CUT TO:

EXT. BILLY'S CAR

Approaching Paris. The tunnel alongside the Seine.

PARIS STREETS - NIGHT

The car, driving along.

EXT. ISOBEL'S APARTMENT BUILDING - NIGHT

The car comes to a stop.

INT. BILLY'S CAR

Billy is in the passenger seat. Isobel has been driving.

                    ISOBEL
          Home.

Billy and Isobel get out.

EXT. CAR - NIGHT

Billy yawns and stretches. Isobel collects her bag.

                    ISOBEL
          That was lovely, Billy. Thank you
          for everything.

She steps forward and kisses him. Then turns to go inside.

                    BILLY
          Wait a minute.

                    ISOBEL
          Yes?

                    BILLY
          May I come in? Have we stopped?
          Moscow... more...

                    ISOBEL
          Billy, we didn't think this
          through. At least, I didn't. But
          on the way back-- It was a wonderful
          weekend. I even enjoyed Arnie. But--

                    BILLY
          We'll do more. We're great together.

                    ISOBEL
          No. it's no good. You're still
          in love with your wife. I don't
          have a good position. You know that.

                    BILLY
          I'm not in love with my wife.
          That's over. I didn't think about
          her once when I was with you. Honest.

                    ISOBEL
          I'm just a distraction. God knows
          I need one, too. But it's not a life.

                    BILLY
          Isobel, I'm crazy about you. I
          could even be in love with you.

                    ISOBEL
          Don't say that. Please.

                    BILLY
          I am not in love with my wife. If
          I never see her again it would be
          perfectly okay with me.

He doesn't sound too convincing.

                    ISOBEL
          And the doll Madame Basquiat gave
          you. What is that?

                    BILLY
          Dumb superstition. Paganism. You
          know I don't believe in that stuff.

                    ISOBEL
          Good night, Billy. If you'd like,
          I can get you another flute teacher.

                    BILLY
          No.

                    ISOBEL
          We have to go back to where we were.

                    BILLY
          That's impossible.

                    ISOBEL
          Then we can't see each other.

                         BILLY
          You didn't let me finish. I'll try.

                         ISOBEL
          I don't want to get hurt. It's
          the way it has to be.

                         BILLY
          Not very romantic.

                         ISOBEL
          I don't like romance. I like--

She turns again, then walks towards the building.

                         BILLY
          What? What do you like?

But she is gone. Billy stands there as we:

                                        CUT TO:

INT. SPA POOL

Billy is swimming back and forth.

INT. LOCKER ROOM

Billy dressing.

EXT. PARIS STREET - DAY

Billy enters a flower shop. Comes out a moment later
carrying a small bouquet.

EXT. ISOBEL'S APARTMENT BUILDING - DAY

Billy enters.

INT. HALLWAY AT ISOBEL'S DOOR

It opens. Isobel admits Billy. He hands her the flowers,
kisses her. She offers a cheek. He is nonplussed, then he
sees a possible explanation. A YOUNG STUDENT is just
packing up.

                    ISOBEL
          Thank you. I'll just put them in
          some water.
                    (to the student; in French)
          [Let yourself out, Alain. I'll
          see you next week.]

Alain leaves. Billy moves into the kitchen where Isobel is
arranging the flowers in a vase. He embraces her. Before
he can get too far, she steps back.

                    ISOBEL
          They really are very lovely.

                    BILLY
          I thought it over. I spent hours
          going over it. From every angle.
          I looked into my heart, my soul,
          my closet. I AM NOT IN LOVE WITH
          MY WIFE ANYMORE. Period. End of
          paragraph, page, book. So help
          me, God!

                    ISOBEL
          I don't believe you, of course.

                    BILLY
          I missed you.

                    ISOBEL
          Billy--

                    BILLY
          That's because it was very
          intense. So it's normal to feel a
          little afraid. But the important
          thing to remember is that we liked
          each other before we fell in love.
          I mean, we're friends, right.
          That's a firm foundation for
          lovers.

                    ISOBEL
          We can't be lovers.

                    BILLY
          We'll find another name. Friends
          who go to bed together because
          they lo-- like each other
          immensely.

                    ISOBEL
          Do you want a flute lesson?

                    BILLY
               (vehemently)
          Of course I want a lesson. That's
          one of the best parts of knowing
          you. How can you even ask me if I
          want a lesson?

                    ISOBEL
          Where's your flute?

                    BILLY
          I forgot it.

Isobel shakes her head.

                                        CUT TO:

EXT. MOVIE THEATRE - NIGHT

Billy and Isobel coming out of the theatre. It has been a
very emotional experience for them and the rest of the
audience, most of whom are drying their eyes. Isobel is no
exception.

Billy and Isobel walk for a bit, not speaking. Suddenly she
stops. Billy faces her. Isobel just starts to cry. Billy
takes her in his arms.

                    ISOBEL
          Oh, Billy. It was so sad.

Billy holds her tenderly.

                    BILLY
          I know. I know.

                                        CUT TO:

INT. A CAFE - LATER THAT NIGHT (MOS)

Billy and Isobel are sharing a huge ice cream creation.
Billy is bubbly and Isobel is laughing, having gotten over
her sadness. She looks at him very kindly.

                                        CUT TO:

INT. BILLY'S APARTMENT - NIGHT

Billy is looking at pictures of Isobel that he took in
Honfleur.

SFX: PHONE RINGS

As Billy talks, he continues to look at the pictures of
Isobel.

INTERCUT

INT. GARAGE - DAY

Arnie Pitkin's Cadillac is on a grease rack. Pitkin is in
the driver's seat shouting into his car phone.

                    PITKIN
          Billy, I'm moving ahead. I spoke
          to somebody very close to Bronson.
          And I told him-- no, not Bronson,
          the guy close to him-- about Lise.
          I want us all to have dinner tonight.

                    BILLY
          Who's the guy?

                    PITKIN
          Not him. You, me, and Lise.

                    BILLY
          I can't tonight, Arnie. I'm busy.

                    PITKIN
          We'll be at La Coupole.

                    BILLY
          You set it up already?

                    PITKIN
          It's her only night free. Billy,
          this is getting close. We have to
          do it. You mind if I meet with
          her alone?

                    BILLY
          Why would I mind?

                    PITKIN
          I don't know. She's too beautiful
          to leave alone with me. Just
          kidding. Maybe you can get out of
          your thing tonight.

                    BILLY
          No way.

                    PITKIN
          Okay. I'll let you know what
          happens.

                    BILLY
          Happens?

                    PITKIN
          Gotta run.

                                        CUT TO:

EXT. PARIS OPERA - NIGHT

Billy rushes up the stairs through the crowd. He spots
Isobel. She takes his arm. They go inside.

INT. OPERA HOUSE

Billy buys a libretto. He turns to Isobel. She looks at him
differently, it seems. She takes a step forward, raises her
hand, and quickly caresses his cheek. She takes his hand
and leads him towards the stairs.

INT. OPERA HOUSE - STAGE

The OVERTURE ENDS. The curtain rises on the first act of
"Tales of Hoffman". The tavern scene.

BILLY AND ISOBEL

Listening, staring at the stage. She moves closer to him.

STAGE

Chorus members fill up the tavern, seated at tables.

BILLY

Something catches his eye. He borrows Isobel's binoculars.

BILLY'S POV THROUGH THE BINOCULARS: A COUPLE sitting at a
table, oblivious to the singing around them. They are
gazing into each other's eyes. The couple, in costume, are
Pitkin and Lise.

BILLY

Rubs his eyes. He can't believe this. He raises the
glasses for another look.

BILLY'S POV THROUGH THE BINOCULARS: Pitkin and Lise are
leaning across the table. They lift their glasses, toast,
and kiss.

BILLY

Rubs his eyes again, blinks, takes another look.

BILLY'S POV: The couple. Not Pitkin and Lise.

BILLY

Relieved, somewhat. He hands the glasses back to Isobel.
As he does, their hands touch. He takes hers, she smiles
and puts her shoulder against his.

OPERA HOUSE HALLWAY

People milling about, smoking, chatting.

BILLY

Holding two glasses of wine, making his way through the
crowd. He finds Isobel where he left her, somewhat near a
potted plant. He hands her a glass of wine. They toast,
then drink. Billy looks at her, he draws her to him, they
kiss easily. Isobel is yielding. Isobel is in love.
Isobel is in trust.

STAGE

We are seeing Act Three. Members of the chorus stand about
in groups or recline on the cushions.

BILLY AND ISOBEL

Enjoying the music. Billy's expression changes. Once
again, the binoculars.

BILLY'S POV: The stage. A couple, stretched out on the
cushions in a passionate embrace. They come up for air.
It's Pitkin and Lise.

BILLY

Lowers the glasses. Clutches his stomach, whispers to Isobel.

                    BILLY
          Stomach... nausea... need some air.

                    ISOBEL
          Shall we leave?

                    BILLY
          No... I'll be fine. I should
          walk... get some air. let's meet
          later. At... Coupole.

                    ISOBEL
          Coupole? Are you all right? I'm
          worried about you.

                    PEOPLE
          Shhhh...

                    BILLY
          I'm fine. I'll be fine. Select.

                    ISOBEL
          What?

                    PEOPLE
          Shhhhhhhhh!

Billy is already leaving.

                    BILLY
                 (whispers)
          Select. Meet you at the Select.

                    ISOBEL
                 (to herself)
          La Coupole...

                                        CUT TO:

EXT. OPERA HOUSE - NIGHT

Billy comes racing down the stairs. Hails a cab.

EXT. LA COUPOLE - NIGHT

The cab stops. Billy gets out and enters the restaurant.

INT. LA COUPOLE

Pitkin and Lise, looking dazzlingly beautiful. Drinking
coffee. Billy walks up to the table.

                    PITKIN
          Hey, Billy. Sit down.

Billy greets Lise and takes a seat.

                    PITKIN
                 (continuing)
          You missed a great meal. What am
          I saying, 'missed'? You can eat.
          I'll get a waiter.

                    BILLY
          Arnie, I'm not here on business.
          Would you excuse us, please?

                    PITKIN
          I'm here on business. You giving
          me the rush?

                    BILLY
          Arnie, could I speak to you alone
          for a minute?

Billy gets up, takes Pitkin aside.

                    PITKIN
          What's going on?

                    BILLY
          I was home. I got a call from her
          father. Her mother-- God, I
          don't know how to tell her.

                    PITKIN
          Oh, Jesus. Poor kid. I'm sorry.
          Listen, I'll take off. Don't
          worry about the check. I'll take
          care of it.

                    BILLY
          Thanks, Arnie.

                    PITKIN
          I'll just say goodbye.

                    PITKIN
          Lise, I enjoyed this. I look
          forward to getting your reaction
          to the script.
                    (then, somberly)
          We all want you. You're a very
          talented woman.

He waves goodbye and exits. A waiter comes over.

                    BILLY
          Coffee. And a cognac.

For a while Lise and Billy just sit and say nothing.
Finally:

                    LISE
          How'd you get rid of Arnie?

                    BILLY
          Does it matter?

                    LISE
                    (shrugs)
          He's exhausting. He says he's got
          Bronson. You, me. The money. Is
          the script any good? Not that I
          can afford to be choosy.

                    BILLY
          No. It's not very good.

                    LISE
          He said it could be rewritten.

                    BILLY
          Lise, don't get your hopes up.

                    LISE
          Why? Don't you want me?

                    BILLY
          Of course I would want you. You'd
          be great. In anything. Arnie's a
          character, but he bullshits. I
          came on strong about using you
          because at the same time it was a
          way-- I thought it was a way to be
          with you. Impress you. Get us
          back together. I would have done
          anything for that to happen.

                    LISE
          And now?

                    BILLY
          It wouldn't do either of us any
          good.

                    LISE
          You sound different, Billy. Like
          you've settled down. You're
          calmer. Calm enough to be honest.

                    BILLY
          I'm the same guy.

                    LISE
          It's like... like you're thinking
          about what's good for me for once.

                    BILLY
          Well, I always thought I was good
          for you.

                    LISE
          Do you still?

Billy is silent. Finally:

                    BILLY
          Maybe it's not the time anymore.

                    LISE
          I don't know how that makes me
          feel.

                    BILLY
          Relieved, I would think.

                    LISE
                 (sadly)
        Yes. Relieved. Of course.

There is another silence. Then:

                    BILLY
        Let me tell you about Bronson.

                                        CUT TO:

EXT. STREET - NIGHT

Isobel walking towards the cafe.

INT. CAFE

BILLY AND LISE (MOS)

Billy talking and Lise laughing.

ISOBEL

Enters the cafe, looking for Billy.

ISOBEL'S POV: BILLY AND LISE

                    LISE
        And he was just fishing?

                    BILLY
        Not in that stream. Never again.

Lise reaches for her purse. Billy puts his hand on hers to
stop her.

ISOBEL'S POV: Billy and Lise "holding hands".

ISOBEL

Turns and walks out of the cafe.

BILLY AND LISE

They get up from the table. Lise seems a bit awkward, as if
there's something she wants to say and can't.

EXT. STREET - NIGHT

They walk for a while, not talking.

> LISE
> Billy, will we be friends?

> BILLY
> I don't know. We can't be less.
> (kisses her)
> I've got to go.

He turns and heads away.

> LISE
> Bye, Billy.

BILLY

Dodging traffic as he crosses the street to The Select.

INT. SELECT - NIGHT

Billy searching, scanning the tables for Isobel. Looks at his watch. Oh, he's very late. No Isobel. He turns and exits.

> CUT TO:

INT. BILLY'S APARTMENT - NIGHT

Billy, on the telephone, waiting for someone to answer. Then:

> ISOBEL
> (filtered)
> Hello.

> BILLY
> It's me. Did you just get home?

> ISOBEL
> (filtered)
> Yes.

> BILLY
> I went to a clinic. I have food poisoning. Nothing serious. They gave me some medicine and I went straight home.

                    ISOBEL
               (filtered)
     I see.

                    BILLY
     So... I tried to call you at the
     Select. You weren't there.

                    ISOBEL
               (filtered)
     I went home.

                    BILLY
     I'm much better now. Shall I come
     over.

                    ISOBEL
               (filtered)
     No.

                    BILLY
     You okay?

                    ISOBEL
               (filtered)
     Yes.

                    BILLY
     I'll see you tomorrow. My lesson.

                    ISOBEL
               (filtered)
     Oh, yes.

                    BILLY
     I'm really sorry about tonight.
               (he really is)
     Can I have a rain check on another
     opera?

                    ISOBEL
               (filtered)
     Rain check?

                    BILLY
     It's an expression. You know,
     when it rains--

                    ISOBEL
              (filtered)
          Billy, I have to hang up. I'm
          very tired. Good night.

We HEAR a click. Billy holds the phone for a moment, then:

                                        CUT TO:

INT. ISOBEL'S APARTMENT - DAY

Billy enters wearing a bandage on his head and playing
"Yankee Doodle Dandy" on the flute.

                    BILLY
          Happy Fourth of July!

Isobel is cool. All business.

                    BILLY
              (continuing)
          Not funny? Oh, well.
              (removes the bandage)
          How about Happy Bastille Day?
              (plays a few bars
               of the Marseilles)
          No?

                    ISOBEL
          How about some long tones?

                    BILLY
              (moving towards her)
          How about a long kiss? An 'a'--
              (reshapes his mouth)
          --an 'o'... but an "os" is not a
          note.

He reaches for her. She backs away. Points to the music
stand.

                    ISOBEL
          Play.

Billy plays a long tone scale. Boring.

                    ISOBEL
              (continuing)
          Next.

Billy, pained, goes on to the quarter note scale, then the eighth note scale. He's getting worse. Then he starts playing "Frère Jacques".

Isobel doesn't find that funny.

                    ISOBEL
          I don't want to teach you anymore.
          To you it's just... fun. I am a
          musician. A serious musician. I
          take this seriously and I expect
          my students to do the same. You
          come here and you make jokes, you
          make tricks, but you don't play
          the goddamn flute. Go somewhere
          else and make jokes.

                    BILLY
          Isobel.

                    ISOBEL
              (pushing him to
               the door)
          Get out. You're a bullshitter...
          like the movies you make. Little
          lies to buy something. You can't
          play the flute with lies. Or
          charm. Get out. Now.

                    BILLY
          What's going on?

                    ISOBEL
          You don't know your scales. You
          don't know anything.

She opens the door and pushes him out into the hallway.

HALLWAY

The door slams. A little boy is sitting on the floor holding his flute case. He's early. Billy looks at him and shrugs.

                              CUT TO:

EXT. PARIS STREETS - DAY

Billy walking, carrying his flute case, very depressed. He
passes the music store where he bought the flute. He
recognizes the place, stops and enters.

INT. MUSIC STORE

The saleman comes up to him.

> SALESMAN
>
> Monsieur?

> BILLY
>
> I was thinking of... returning it.

> SALESMAN
>
> Is it defective?

> BILLY
>
> No. It's just that it's a very
> hard instrument.

The salesman gives him an expression of "not my problem".

> BILLY
> (continuing)
>
> So, I suppose... would you... my
> money back?

The salesman shakes his head "not a chance".

> BILLY
> (continuing)
>
> What now?

> SALESMAN
>
> Practice. There is no other way.
> You must practice.

> CUT TO:

EXT. FRANK'S APARTMENT - NIGHT

We see Frank arrive with JASMINE, a model.

INT. FRANK'S BEDROOM - NIGHT

Frank and Jasmine are in a passionate embrace, about to
disrobe totally.

Suddenly, they HEAR Billy playing long notes on the flute.

                    JASMINE
          That's... that's... a flute.

With that, Jasmine's mood goes completely to pieces. She
bursts into tears, half-dressed as she is, and begins
sobbing on the bed.

                    FRANK
          I'll tell him to stop. Why are
          you crying?

                    JASMINE
          My mother... my mother always
          played scales just like that on
          the flute. So beautiful...

Frank tears out of the room.

INT. LIVING ROOM - NIGHT

Billy is solemnly playing the scales.

                    FRANK
          Enough!

Billy blinks innocently.

Jasmine comes sniffling out of the bedroom.

                    JASMINE
          No, no, no... go on!

Frank slaps his forehead with exasperation. Billy resumes
the scales. Jasmine watches adoringly from the couch,
sobbing her heart out at the same time.

                                        CUT TO:

EXT. FRANK'S APARTMENT - NIGHT

Billy is leaving Frank's house carrying a suitcase.

EXT. HOTEL - NIGHT

WE HEAR Billy playing scales. The lights in the hotel go on
here and there and WE HEAR people yelling and banging on
walls, doors, etc.

But scales go on and on through the next scene.

EXT. HOTEL FRONT DOOR - NIGHT

Billy leaving, carrying his suitcase.

EXT. SOPHIE'S PLACE - NIGHT

WE HEAR scales continue as Billy rings Sophie's front door.
She opens the door in her nightgown. She was sleeping.

INT. SOPHIE'S PLACE - GUEST ROOM - NIGHT

Sophie shows him a small room. He goes in, shuts the door,
erects a music stand and he is again playing.

INT. SOPHIE'S BEDROOM

Sophie puts in earplugs.

EXT. APARTMENT BUILDING - DAY

The music goes on, the melody becoming more and more
sophisticated. Sophie and Billy are standing in the street
outside this apartment house.

INT. FURNISHED APARTMENT

As the MUSIC CONTINUES, Sophie shows Billy this nice
apartment. Billy puts his suitcase down, plugs in his
answering machine, and starts in playing again. He plays
extremely well.

OTHER INSTRUMENTS JOIN IN.

                                        CUT TO:

CLOSEUP - FLUTE

Camera PULLS BACK to reveal that Billy is playing in a
symphony orchestra. A flute concerto. He's wearing a
tuxedo. At the end of the concerto, the audience applauds
frantically. Isobel is in the first row, applauding and
looking very happy.

SUDDENLY WE HEAR the RING of a phone.

The fantasy stops.

                                        CUT TO:

INT. BILLY'S NEW APARTMENT - NIGHT

Billy picks up the ringing phone.

                    BILLY
                (into phone)
          Lise? Lunch? Oh, lunch... No, no
          I can't go out. I'm staying here.
          Oh, okay. I'll... goodbye.

EXT. ISOBEL'S APARTMENT

Billy is standing outside Isobel's door, playing the flute.

No one answers. He knocks. There is no reaction. He
knocks again, and resumes playing the flute.

A NEIGHBOR comes out.

                    NEIGHBOR
          C'est très beau, mais elle n'est
          pas là.

                    BILLY
          Pas là?

                    NEIGHBOR
          Non. Elle a un concert à
          Royaumont
                    BILLY
          Royaumont?

                    NEIGHBOR
          Oui.

The neighbor goes back inside, leaving Billy stranded with
his flute in the hallway. Billy takes out a notepad and
writes a note down... his new phone number and address. He
slips the note under Isobel's door.

EXT. ISOBEL'S APARTMENT BUILDING - DAY

Billy stands by his car for a moment, not certain of what to
do. Then he gets in the car.

EXT. ROAD ENTERING ROYAUMONT

Billy drives into town.

EXT. CONCERT HALL

Billy enters.

INT. CONCERT HALL

We see Billy walk to the front of the auditorium where he
squeezes past people to a single seat.

Isobel is about to begin playing a concerto. The conductor
raises his baton. Isobel sees Billy. She comes in a
fraction later than she should.

There's a slight reaction from the conductor.

INT. BACKSTAGE

After the concert, Billy sees Isobel talking with other
musicians. She sees Billy, and turns away, trying to
be more immersed in conversation.

Undaunted, Billy approaches her.

                    BILLY
          Hello, Isobel.

                    ISOBEL
               (cool)
          Billy.

                    BILLY
          It was wonderful. You were
          wonderful, all of you. Isobel...
          could we talk?

                    ISOBEL
          I'm busy.

                    BILLY
          Please.

She shrugs and goes with him a little away from the crowd.

                    BILLY
          Listen, I've been practicing my
          scales day and night and I--

                    ISOBEL
          It's not the damn scales, you...
          you... It's you. With <u>her</u> at
          La Coupole!!

                    BILLY
          Oh... I can explain that.

                    ISOBEL
          No, please don't. I don't want to
          hear any more lies. You're still
          in love with her. And she
          probably still loves you. You
          should go back with her. And
          leave me alone!

                    BILLY
          But we...

With that, she turns on her heel and plunges into a group of
musicians, leaving Billy hoisted on his own petard.

INT. AMPHITHEATRE - NEXT DAY

We watch the musicians rehearse a difficult passage. The
conductor puts down his baton, the players relax. Some light
cigarettes, some sip coffee, some chat.

When suddenly WE HEAR the sound of a flute. A scale in
quarter notes, played perfectly.

ANGLE - BILLY

Standing at the rear of the amphitheatre, playing.

THE ORCHESTRA

The musicians look at him. Isobel is befuddled. She
doesn't know what to do.

He reaches the last note and holds it triumphantly.

BILLY

Lowers his flute to the musicians' APPLAUSE.

Billy stands still for a moment, then, slowly and with great
dignity, bows. Then he turns and walks out.

INT. BILLY'S APARTMENT - NIGHT

Billy is listening to music, sitting in a chair. He picks
up his flute and fingers the keys without playing. He puts
it down, picks it up again, raises it to his lips and finds
a note to fit the final chord of the record. The music
ends, his note continues, solitary and sad.

                                        CUT TO:

EXT. LUXEMBOURG GARDEN - DAY

Billy, Lise, and Butch (the dog) are walking. Butch carries
the voodoo doll in his mouth. Lise has Billy's arm. He
seems pre-occupied. She concentrates on him. Their
situation has come full circle.

Billy stops, faces Lise.

                    BILLY
          No. I don't think you made a
          mistake. I think you did what was
          right for you at the time. And
          the funny thing is that it was
          right for me, too. I just didn't
          know it then.

                    LISE
          Billy, I think I still love you.

                         BILLY
          But that doesn't mean we should be
          together. I'll always love you,
          too, Lise. But our lives are
          meant to take different paths.
          Exciting, wonderful paths.

                         LISE
          I'm starting to feel a lot of
          pain, Billy. Was that what it was
          like for you?

                         BILLY
          It will go away, Lise.

He bends down and takes the doll out of Butch's mouth and
puts it in his pocket.

                         BILLY
                    (continuing)
          I promise. You'll see.

He hugs her, comforting her.

                         LISE
          I hope so, Billy. I hope so.

                                        CUT TO:

EXT. HONFLEUR - DAY

Billy, a large notebook in hand, is walking along the
waterfront. It's a cold, grey day. The tourists are gone.
The boats knock against each other gently in the wind.

EXT. HONFLEUR BEACH - DAY

Billy walks along the beach.

BILLY

Looking out at the sea.

                                        CUT TO:

EXT. HONFLEUR BEACH - DAY

Billy, sitting on the rocks. He is writing in his notebook.

                    BILLY (V.O.)
          When my wife and I got separated,
          I was neurotic, destructive,
          jealous, obsessive, and rude. The
          whole time I thought I was a
          perfect gentleman.

Billy pauses. He looks out at the sea.

There is a sudden gust of wind and a few loose pages fly
away.

Billy rushes after them to gather them up. As he bends down
to pick up the last one, he notices a woman at a short
distance, facing him. He looks up. It is Isobel. No, it
cannot be. It must be one of his fantasies again.

He walks away, then stops. Hesitates, and looks back. It
really is Isobel.

He runs towards her. As they are about to embrace, Arnie
Pitkin's VOICE is heard, yelling at a distance. Billy and
Isobel freeze.

                    PITKIN (O.C.)
          Hey, Billy! Where the hell have
          you been? We've got Bronson! I
          spoke to him! We've got Bronson!

Billy takes Isobel's hand and together, they run off.

                                        FADE OUT.

                    THE END